in every human being. I commend it to everyone, but especially to seminarians and the ministers of the next generation."

—**Wm. Dwight McKissic, Sr,**
senior pastor, Cornerstone Baptist Church, Arlington, TX

"He is insightful, biblical, prophetic, and engaging with his encouragement and challenges to the reader. This book is being released in the middle of a racial reckoning, a mental health pandemic, and global health pandemic. The timing of this release could only have been arranged by God. It's a book that I believe will give vocal cords and a voice back to the marginalized and oppressed by way of the pulpit heralder and the hearers of the pew. It also places tools in the hands of others that make the work doable for all people."

—**Cokiesha Bailey Robinson,** founder, Cross Spring Ministries,
and associate dean of student diversity, Grace College

"*Social Crisis Preaching* is a textbook that addresses inequities and injustice in our world by viewing them through a redemptive lens based upon the biblical text. In a day when the tendency is to assign the biblical text to a secondary function or role, Dr. Gardner connects social crisis preaching to its primary source: the Bible. In this work, the ancient scriptural text gives voice to the contemporary social texture so that the fruit and the root, the cure and the cause, the consequent and the antecedent, are held in unrelinquishable tension. The book is saturated in a Christological solution, thus offering the only way society and its members can be redeemed to Christ."

—**Robert Smith,** Charles T. Carter Baptist Chair of Divinity and professor of Christian Preaching, Beeson Divinity School at Samford University

"In this wonderful book, Gardner contends that the preaching of the gospel necessarily involves the preaching about crises in society. Sin has marred humanity and created the social conditions which dehumanize human beings. The gospel is the healing salve that abrogates the corruptive powers of sin. Real gospel preaching, then, mandates addressing the source and symptoms of sin in order to overturn its authority in the world. I highly recommend this book to anyone concerned about preaching the truth of Jesus Christ without compromise."

—**Ralph Douglas West,** senior pastor, The Church Without Walls, Houston, TX

"As a pastor and an academic in the Deep South for nearly 20 years, Dr. Tyshawn Gardner has written a guide for preachers interested in 'social crisis preaching.' His practical illustrations and sample outlines will be a helpful guide for preachers who will dare to address, from the biblical texts, some of the challenging social crises of our day. Even when readers disagree with Dr. Gardner's method, suggestions, and conclusions, they will still learn."

—**Jarvis J. Williams,** associate professor of New Testament interpretation,
The Southern Baptist Theological Seminary

SOCIAL CRISIS PREACHING

To: Dr. Andre Kirkland,

preach the word, stand with
the poor, defend the weak, Glory
God!

With gratitude

06/13/2023

TYSHAWN GARDNER

SOCIAL CRISIS PREACHING

BIBLICAL PROCLAMATION
for **TROUBLED TIMES**

ACADEMIC
BRENTWOOD, TENNESSEE

Dedicated to my loving mother, Ednar Joyce Gardner,
who introduced me to Jesus Christ,
then showed me His love and courage through her life.

CONTENTS

ACKNOWLEDGMENTS

am appreciative to countless people who encouraged me in writing this important book. It has been demanding and humbling. It is a blessing to write about one's passion and interest. I am thankful to God for the call to preach the gospel of Jesus Christ and for the opportunity to care for and to train pastors, preachers, and leaders. There is no higher calling or greater joy than the sacred obligation of proclaiming the transformative truths of the Word of God.

I am grateful to Broadman and Holman Academic for trusting me with the serious task of writing about preaching. Madison Trammel, Michael McEwen, and Jessi Wallace have been patient, kind, and extremely helpful and encouraging. Their work is a blessing and vitally important to the academy and the church.

I owe thanks to my pastors and mentors, Frank Kennedy, Jr. and Frank Kennedy, Sr. Their lives have been an example to me of Christian ethics and integrity. Their preaching and counsel have impacted my life in multiple dimensions that are yet unfolding. I am thankful to my teacher, mentor, and chief supporter, Robert Smith, Jr. Dr. Smith encourages my soul, while he challenges my mind to commit to excellence; without both, this book would not be possible nor conceivable. I am also thankful for my friends, Pastor Freddie Robertson and Pastor Greg Morris, who constantly show themselves friendly and who pray for me with or without my request. Special thanks to Samuel Hagos, who is my student, teacher, friend, and brother. Thank you for your help with this manuscript.

My wife and children have sacrificed the most for this project. Their patience and understanding allowed me the space, time, and peace I needed to work. My family is my greatest joy and my deepest source of joy and happiness. I am thankful for my wife, children, and grandchildren. The thought of them motivated every keystroke, as I was reminded of how blessed I am to be entrusted with such a beautiful blessing. My wife, Shonetay, and our children, Coretta, Tristan, and Titus, our son in law, Rev. Corey Savage, along with our grandchildren, Ayla, Carter, and Brenna strengthen me with their love and their lives. I am also indebted to my beautiful mother-in-law, Estella Edwards, who loves me like her own and has invested in my ministry from day one. Her Christian love and service to her family reminds me of our responsibility to sacrificial service. She is the quintessential example of generosity and dedication.

My parents, Edward and Ednar Gardner, support me in adulthood as fiercely as they supported me in all my childhood endeavors. They have gone to the ends of the earth for their children, and their sacrifices for my brothers and I are an example of unconditional love. This book is dedicated to my mother. She not only introduced me to Jesus Christ, but she insisted that I attend and participate in church. She discipled me and made my spiritual life her priority. She taught me, that in all life's crises, to seek shelter and solace in the Word of God and its Author. I love you, Mama.

INTRODUCTION:

TOWARDS AN ETHIC OF SOCIAL CRISIS PREACHING

I am an avid sports fan. I spend many Saturday afternoons with remote control, lemon pepper wings, and Dr. Pepper in tow, watching the competitive fierceness of college basketball or football games. As entertaining as the games are, the hilarious commercials shown during the time-outs and halftime are equally engaging. During the 2019 NCAA March Madness men's basketball tournament, AT&T launched a year-long set of "Just OK Is Not OK" commercials to promote their 4K network. Their goal was to help customers see that "just OK" network coverage is not merely "OK." But the commercials struck a deeper chord with me. Each commercial presents ordinary life situations, like taking your car to a mechanic, sitting in a doctor's office, or hiring a babysitter. While every case is relatable yet unique, the common thread in the series is that the characters sought assurance, certainty, and guarantee in each predicament.

My favorite commercial in the series features a man in a hospital preparing for a procedure, when his wife, who is at his bedside, asks the attending nurse, "Have you ever worked with Dr. Francis?" The nurse replies, "Oh yeah, he's OK," to which the patient with a grimace on his face, trepidatiously interjects, "Just OK?" The next scene has a very nonchalant, head-in-the-clouds Dr. Francis strolling into the hospital room as he rhetorically asks, "Guess who just got reinstated, well, not officially?" The commercial then fades to the narrator who says, "Just OK is not OK."

The social crisis preacher proclaims the justice and hope of the gospel in a world where "just OK is not OK." These five words bear prophetic witness to the times in which we live. Social crisis preaching addresses a world where the "OK-ness" of the social order has become accepted as the norm. It disturbs and upends the milieu of those who are "OK" with things being "OK." This "just OK" mentality of callousness and numbness breeds nihilism, where little compassion is shown for those in dire situations, who cry, "This is not OK!" This apathy is an anti-gospel, deadening spirit that prohibits the fruit of the Spirit from sprouting and growing in our lives (Matt 7:16; Luke 13:6–9; Gal 5:22–23).

Social crisis preaching is *biblically rooted, Spirit-enabled proclamation that develops and drives congregations to compassionately care for and radically confront social crises in the communities where their neighbors live, work, worship, and play.* Think of the twelve-year-old girl taken captive by the ever-growing, multimillion-dollar-per-day human trafficking industry. This is not OK. There are more payday and title lenders in Alabama than hospitals, high schools, movie theaters, and county courthouses combined, driving the five thousand people per day who take out these loans deeper into financial crisis.[1] This is not OK. Imagine the ambitious, gifted children who are told to dream big (and they do). But they are also assigned to ghettos, where failing schools, bleak job opportunities, subpar healthcare systems, and underfunded social services all align to ensure that the cycle of poverty continues deep into succeeding generations. This is not OK. Social crisis preaching addresses big pharma, politicians, and the wealthy investors of pharmaceutical companies who allow opioids to ravage middle-class communities and destroy young couples' lives. Seeing tens of thousands of Americans die from opioid abuse is not OK. Preachers who engage in social crisis preaching have a responsibility to address the threats of national security,

> Social crisis preaching is *biblically rooted, Spirit-enabled proclamation that develops and drives congregations to compassionately care for and radically confront social crises in the communities where their neighbors live, work, worship, and play.*

[1.] Alabama Appleseed Center for Law and Justice and Alabama Arise, "Broke: How Payday Lenders Crush Alabama Communities," 4, accessed February 10, 2022. https://www.alabamaappleseed.org/wp-content/uploads/2019/04/Alabama-Appleseed-BROKE-Report-Web.pdf.

foreign wars, and the psychological and emotional toll that international conflicts exact on the brave women and men who serve the nation. These daily realities are not OK. When there is political corruption on every level, the ugly monster of voter suppression arises, and policymakers lobby for the wealthy and not for the poor, this is not OK. Imagine the elderly couple who faithfully worked thirty-plus years, purchased their home, put their children through school, and served their community with pride, only to see that same community now ravaged with drugs, gang violence, and shark real estate developers. This is not OK. Although there are pockets of improvement and promise related to how Christianity has positively influenced national policies towards minorities, the poor, and the most vulnerable, one cursory glance at the spiritual and social conditions of our communities and our nation tells us that things are "just OK." But alas, "just OK is not OK."

A social crisis is a disordered condition within a community that disrupts people's *shalom* (peace) and flourishing. Social crisis preaching addresses a multitude of social realities that have reached crisis mode, yet many of these social crises are structural and systemic. Avid social media users, self-proclaimed scholars, and mainstream media pundits, loosely, and sometimes irresponsibly, use terms that further divide people into opposing camps. Clear definitions and examples must guide our conversations about systemic and institutional injustices.

Systemic racism is a term that generally generates much discussion and disagreement. Renowned scholar, Joe R. Feagin defines systemic racism:

> The unjustly gained socioeconomic resources and assets of whites, and the long-term maintenance of major socioeconomic inequalities across what came to be defined as a rigid color line . . . . Systemic racism encompasses a broad range of white-racist dimensions: the racist ideology, attitudes, emotions, habits, actions, and institutions of whites in this society.[2]

Feagin rightly explains that racism transcends the mere "feelings" of dislike held by members of one racial group towards another. Racism

---

[2] Joe R. Feagin, *Systemic Racism: A Theory of Oppression* (New York: Routledge, 2006), 2.

indeed includes feelings of bias, but it also involves power and affects people economically.

Noted sociologists Michael Emerson and Christian Smith report that a racialized society and the causes of racial division can be seen in these aspects of society: "(1) are increasingly covert, (2) are embedded in normal operations of institutions, (3) avoid direct racial terminology, and (4) are invisible to most Whites."[3] Smith and Emerson's definition of a racialized society will be of paramount importance throughout the course of this text as we discuss the responsibility of the social crisis preacher as sacred anthropologist in serving as a resource for the people in the pews. Racism is just as prevalent today as it was in 1962; this sin is still among us. Even though the blatant "whites only" markers are absent from stores, movie theaters, government offices, private businesses, education, and worship, the brokenness of humanity makes racism and all its vicissitudes a daily reality for many.

Closely associated with systemic racism is the term *systemic or institutional injustice.* This term is used to define the political, social, economic, health, and educational structures that create inequity in resources and access to opportunities. Those dedicated to eradicating institutional injustices assert that there are policies, laws, and rules that adversely affect one group of image-bearers more than another, even if inequity is not the intention. Consider the incalculable amount of wealth African Americans lost due to the government laws and policies that made housing discrimination acceptable and normal. Richard Rothstein, in his award-winning work *The Color of Law: A Forgotten History of How Our Government Segregated America,* observes, "An account of *de jure* residential segregation has to include not only how public policy geographically separated African Americans from whites but also how federal and state labor market policies, with undisguised racial intent, depressed African American wages. In addition, some and perhaps many local governments taxed African Americans more heavily than whites."[4]

Feagin, in another seminal text, elaborates on one of the specific hallmarks of institutionalized injustice, "Another common frame notion

---

[3] Michael O. Emerson and Christian Smith, *Divided by Faith: Evangelical Religion and the Problem of Race in America* (New York: Oxford, 2000), 9.

[4] Richard Rothstein, *The Color of Law: A Forgotten History of How Our Government Segregated America* (New York: Liveright, 2017), 154.

views local bureaucratic organizations such as a public school or government agency as properly white-controlled, white-normed, and/or slanted toward white interests."[5] Respected Christian legal scholar and attorney Bryan Stevenson's work at the Equal Justice Initiative is noteworthy in the area of systemic or institutional injustice. One instance of systemic injustice is found in the criminal courts and jury selection. The Equal Justice Initiative reports, "A recent study in Mississippi spanning a 25–year period ending in 2017 found that Black prospective jurors were four times more likely to be struck than white prospective jurors. Similarly, an analysis of more than 5,000 Louisiana cases from 2011 to 2017 found that prosecutors struck black jurors at 175% the expected rate based on their proportion of the jury pool."[6] These biased jury selections have resulted in countless excessive sentences, wrongful convictions, and in some cases, even death sentences and executions.

Perhaps no other work provides a clearer portrait of systemic injustice than Harriet A. Washington's groundbreaking text *Medical Apartheid: The Dark History of Medical Experimentation on Black Americans from Colonial Times to the Present*. Washington states

> The much-bewailed racial health gap is not a gap, but a chasm wider and deeper than a mass grave. The gulf has riven our nation so dramatically that it appears as if we were considering the health profiles of people in two different countries—a medial apartheid.[7]

Social crisis preachers should not only be concerned with how these atrocities affect image-bearers, but they should also bring the gospel of Christ to bear on these kinds of injustices through expository, thematic, and narrative preaching.[8]

[5.] Joe R. Feagin, *The White Racial Frame: Centuries of Racial Framing and Counter-Framing* (New York: Routledge, 2013), 141.

[6.] See, Equal Justice Initiative, "Race and the Jury: Illegal Discrimination in Jury Selection," chap. 4. accessed January 29, 2022. https://eji.org/report/race-and-the-jury/. See also https://www.prisonpolicy.org/scans/reprieve_australia/Blackstrikes_Caddo_Parish_August_2015.pdf.

[7.] Harriet A. Washington, *Medial Apartheid: The Dark History of Medical Experimentation on Black Americans from Colonial Times to the Present* (New York: Anchor, 2010), 20.

[8.] For more scholarly readings on systemic racism and institutional injustices of various manifestations see: Michelle Alexander, *The New Jim Crow: Mass Incarceration in the Age of Colorblindness* (New York: The New Press, 2010); Doris Marie Provine, *Unequal Under Law: Race in the War on Drugs* (Chicago: University of Chicago, 2007); Carol Anderson, *The Second: Race and Guns in a*

This is a homiletics textbook that promotes hermeneutical, exegetical, and homiletical responsibility in moving from text to sermon in social crisis proclamation. It also argues for social crisis preaching as a pastoral responsibility for making disciples who will respond with radical mercy, justice, and Christian love to address the crises confronting their own communities and those of their neighbors. Part 1 provides an ethic of social crisis preaching (chapter 1) and a pastoral theology that gives insight for understanding those who hear our preaching (chapter 2).

Part 2 will instruct the social crisis preacher on how to move from theory to practice, text to sermon, and theology to application—the nuts and bolts of social crisis proclamation.[9] In both parts, I will introduce social crisis preaching as the act of proclamation God uses to expose sin in its varying forms, to promote the hope of Christ, and to realign God's creation closer to his intended vision for humanity.

A DEFINITION OF SOCIAL CRISIS PREACHING

Kelly Miller Smith, Sr. is one of only thirteen African Americans to deliver Yale University's distinguished Lyman Beecher Lectures. In his 1983 lecture, entitled "Social Crisis Preaching," he defines social crisis preaching as "the proclamation of that which is crucially relevant within the context of the Christian gospel in times of social upheaval and stress."[10] In this definition, Smith Sr. solidifies social crisis preaching as Christian proclamation rooted in the Bible. Furthermore, Smith Sr.'s definition implies that the content in the gospel is sufficiently relevant to address contemporary social crises.

An acknowledgement of what is meant by a "social issue" or "crisis" is also in order. Ronald J. Allen defines what constitutes a social issue. He writes

---

Fatally Unequal America (New York: Bloomsbury, 2021); Ta-Nehisi Coates, "The Case for Reparations," *Atlantic*, June 2014, https://www.theatlantic.com/magazine/archive/2014/06/the-case-for-reparations/361631/; Isabel Wilkerson, *Caste: The Origins of Our Discontents* (New York: Random, 2020); Rebecca Skloot, *The Immortal Life of Henrietta Lacks* (New York: Broadway, 2010).

[9.] I will use "social crisis preaching" and "social crisis proclamation" as synonymous terms throughout the book.

[10.] Kelly Miller Smith, Sr. *Social Crisis Preaching: The Lyman Beecher Lectures, 1983* (Macon, GA: Mercer University, 1983), 33.

I consider a social issue to have the following characteristics. It is public. People are aware of it, or should be aware of it. The issue affects the community as a community, that is, it creates social consequences. It affects the well-being of the society. Many social issues are systemic. Social issues may call for the community to invoke a common understanding or behavior in light of the issue.[11]

Smith Sr.'s definition of social crisis preaching, when viewed through the lens of Allen's definition of a social issue with his emphasis on "community," implies that all social crises are communal concerns. Social crisis preaching challenges the church, in times of "social upheaval and stress," to raise the question, "Who is my neighbor?" (Luke 10:29). "Social upheaval and stress" should "affect the community as a community"; however, too often social crises are isolated to certain communities. A part of social crisis preaching then is addressing the root causes and the fruit of why we seldom live "as a community."

In my definition of social crisis preaching, I lead preachers and churches to embody Jesus's admonition to "love your neighbor as yourself" (Mark 12:31). In this way, I define social crisis preaching as "biblically rooted, Spirit-enabled proclamation that develops and drives congregations to compassionately care for and radically confront social crises in the communities where their neighbors live, work, worship, and play." Social crisis preaching consistently provides clear sermonic application, calling for congregations to love God and their neighbor by caring for their neighbor's mental, spiritual, and physical well-being. This proclamation might challenge the ideological constructs that foster hate and division among racial groups.

In similar fashion, social crisis preaching may prompt a congregation to consider how they might leverage their influence and power in the advocacy for more green space, well-lit streets, and improved infrastructure for children who live and play in high-crime areas. Social crisis preaching calls congregations to act with redemptive compassion towards the formerly incarcerated by ensuring that they have a loving church where they can hear the gospel and serve, opportunities to earn a livable wage, access to educational opportunities, and a place to live. If we model the

---

[11.] Ronald J. Allen, "Preaching on Social Issues," *Encounter* 59, no. 1/2 (1998): 59.

Lord's example in Luke 4:18, ministry to the formerly incarcerated is a field ripe with opportunities. Yet the laborers are few. These image-bearers, many who professed faith in Christ in prison and turned their life around, once released, are excluded from employment and housing. The federal and state laws that govern their lives ensure that once they are released, their bondage continues. Reuben Jonathan Miller testifies

> Housing-application denials for people with criminal records doubled in the first six months after Clinton's address.[12] By 1998, almost every public-housing authority in the nation had taken up some version of the initiative, barring people with criminal records form the premises and evicting entire families who let formerly incarcerated loved ones sleep on their couches. Exclusion became official housing policy.[13]

Social crisis preaching also proclaims God's love in Christ for those who are lost and who futilely seek identity in worldly pleasures, material possessions, and empty ambitions. In this definition, not only is social crisis preaching defined as biblical proclamation, but there are two ways in which it is also communal. First, it develops the local congregation to become the community that models justice, love, and mercy. These sermons move congregations to stand with others in spaces like school board meetings, where they advocate for qualified teachers and adequately equipped facilities that are safe and prepare children for educational and career opportunities. Social crisis preaching calls for clear sermonic application that tethers our treatment of neighbor to our baptism and confessions of faith. The confession to love neighbor as one's self requires that we "do unto others as we would have them to do unto you" (Luke 6:31). This sermonic application tying the

---

[12.] President Bill Clinton, January 23, 1996, State of the Union address. Clinton challenged landlords to evict tenants who commit crimes. The Department of Housing and Urban Development also implemented strict public housing policies that required eviction of residents who committed crimes. Congress passes the Housing Opportunity Extension Act of 1996, that required public-housing agencies to evict tenants who committed crimes and to evict tenants who have guests who had previously been convicted of crimes. See Clinton's address, accessed February 4, 2022. https://clintonwhitehouse4.archives.gov/WH/New/other/sotu.html.

[13.] Reuben Jonathan Miller, *Halfway Home: Race, Punishment, and the Afterlife of Mass Incarceration* (New York: Little, Brown, and Co., 2021), 175.

foundational principles of our faith to concrete social acts may mean demanding that local governments support struggling small businesses through tax-breaks, grants, and other incentives that will empower the employees and owners of those businesses.

Second, it introduces God's vision of humanity to communities beset by injustice. The social crisis sermon calls communities to respond to God's redemptive grace and love for his creation by taking responsibility for cleaning up their own communities from drugs and crime, while also calling out corporate greed and government neglect. Social crisis preaching calls attention to the finished work of Christ on the cross and the empowering and enabling power of the Holy Spirit to eradicate hate from the hearts of racists and those who practice other forms of bigotry.

Thus, social crisis preaching prevents congregations from being myopic in their limited views of social issues, selfishly only caring about and confronting the crises that threaten them personally. My definition of social crisis preaching also avoids the humanistic efforts that preachers and congregations often use when addressing society's most controversial issues. It does so by tethering the practice of preaching and the congregation's application to the power of the Holy Spirit for its effectiveness.

THE SUFFICIENCY OF THE TOTALITY OF THE GOSPEL

Some seek to avoid social crisis preaching. To them, "the gospel" is defined in nonsocial terms, only focusing on the spiritual—the rebirth, fellowship, and new heaven and new earth. But the true gospel unites and liberates. It addresses sin in every area of our pedestrian human position. The gospel may unite us in relational love and agreement on the most foundational theological tenets, but it does not mean that liberation from social and cultural strongholds is a realization for all. Christina Barland Edmonson and Chad Brennan instruct, "Contrary to popular belief, the Bible does not teach that our relational dynamics with one another are separate from the gospel, a distraction from the gospel, or a much lower priority than the gospel."[14] Racial justice and equality is also the

---

[14.] Christina Barland Edmondson and Chad Brennan, *Faithful Anti-Racism: Moving Past Talk to Systemic Change,* (Downers Grove, IL: InterVarsity, 2022), 36.

gospel. The totality of the gospel means liberation. Social crisis preaching recaptures and reclaims what it means to be liberated. Liberation, as both a word and a concept, has deep biblical roots and is a major aspect in the ethics of Christian theology and ministry. Paul, in his letter to the Galatians, contends that Jesus Christ "gave himself for our sins to deliver us from the present evil age, according to the will of our God and Father" (Gal 1:4 ESV). By "the present evil age," Paul is suggesting that the death of Christ brought radical implications to salvation, thus loosening sin's grip in all historical and social realities. Timothy George explains how Christ's death has spiritual and social implications:

> The coming of Christ has drastically relativized, though not completely obliterated, former distinctions of race, class, and gender. It also has placed in a totally new perspective such former requirements as circumcision, food laws, and feast days. Christ has rescued us from this present evil age through justifying us by faith and pouring out his Spirit in our lives.[15]

The liberation that social crisis preaching proclaims permeates the spiritual and the social. This liberation is first and foremost a spiritual liberation from the eternal effects of all sin, by and because of, the atoning sacrifice of Jesus on the cross.

This spiritual liberation in Christ transforms the dehumanizing social, political, and economic structures that bind humanity to the sinful realities of the fall. Women and men, as new creatures in Christ, must advocate for and build a world that consistently reflects the glory of God and his intention for his creation. In short, there is no liberation apart from the transforming power of the cross and resurrection of Christ. The purpose of God's redemptive act in his Son was (and is) to liberate people from sin and reconcile them to God. Hugo Magallanes rightly states

> God's liberation is intrinsically connected to the creation narrative, in which all aspects of the human being and society are crafted in perfect harmony, and to the eschatological images of the book of Revelation, in which the promise of perfect harmony comes

---

[15.] Timothy George, *Galatians*, Vol. 30 (Nashville: B&H, 1994), 87.

to fruition. Then, the "in-between" time is precisely God's call to liberate—that is, to resemble the perfect harmony described at the beginning and at the end of the biblical narrative. God's liberation, then, encompasses all aspects of the human being and all elements of the universe and society.[16]

Sin seeks to destroy, bind, and distort every person or entity it infiltrates. Because sin knows no boundaries, it affects every aspect of our being—our thinking, decision-making, and actions (Jer 17:9; Mark 7:22; Eph 4:22; Rom 1:21, 12:1–2). Sinful individuals create sinful ideologies, structures, and systems that cause harm and dysfunction in society (Exod 1:8–14; Dan 3:1–7; Matt 23:1–4; Luke 23:6–25; Jas 5:1–6). God intervenes to restore and bring wholeness by liberating humanity through the cross of Christ, where sin and death are defeated.

It is here where a brief critique of the pros and cons of liberation theology is most needed. The Rev. Dr. James Hal Cone is considered the father of Black liberation theology. Even though Cone did not coin the term Black liberation theology, nor was he the first African American to write a theology of liberation directed towards the Black experience in America and the diaspora, his influence is undeniable.[17] Cone and other Black liberation theologians brought the Bible to bear on racism and racial violence; they brought an indictment on the silence from white Christians and white churches towards those realities. James Cone rightly observes

---

[16.] Hugo Magallanes, "Liberation," in *Dictionary of Scripture and Ethics*, ed. Joel B. Green (Grand Rapids: Baker, 2011), 481.

[17.] The term *Black theology* was coined by a group of forty-eight of the most influential Black clergy across the country who drafted a statement in 1966 entitled "Black Power," which was published as a full-page ad in the *New York Times* in 1966. See James Cone and Gayraud S. Wilmore, *Black Theology: A Documentary History, Volume One: 1966–1979* (Maryknoll, NY: Orbis), 19–26. Cone states in his book *For My People: Black Theology and the Black Church, Where Have We Been and Where Are We Going?* (Maryknoll, NY: Orbis, 1991), that there are three reasons Black theology emerged as a viable rationale. First, the civil rights movement as defined by Martin Luther King, Jr. during the 1950s and 1960s. Second, as a response to Joseph R. Washington in Washington's book *Black Religion: The Negro and Christianity in the United States* (Boston, Beacon, 1964). Washington argued that Black churches are not real churches, since they neither practice the true religion found in white churches, where they were not welcomed. Since Black people were excluded from white churches, where true theology was found, Black churches were not real churches; since any church without a theology is not a church. The third reason Black theology was popularized was due to the influence of the Black power movement and Black nationalist groups, led by leaders such as Malcolm X.

All creative theologies come into being as persons encounter contradictions in life about which they cannot be silent. The same was
true of the appearance of black theology in the 1960s. As Martin
Luther could not remain silent about indulgences in the Catholic Church, and as Karl Barth could not remain silent about the
inordinate confidence of liberal theology in human goodness, so
black theologians could not remain silent about the ever-increasing
manifestations of racism in the white church and its theology.[18]

Latin American as well as Black liberation theologies arose because
of the existing contradictions between the social, ethical, moral, and
economic practices of the church and the Bible's clear teachings on
love, unity, and justice.

Among other positive theological contributions in liberation theologies, social crisis preaching appreciates African American liberation
theology's biblical response to systemic racism and sinful structures.
Feagin reminds us that systemic racism is "the unjustly gained socioeconomic resources and assets of whites, and the long-term maintenance of major socioeconomic inequalities across what came to be
defined as a rigid color line."[19] Liberation theologies have championed
the poor and emphasized Jesus's care and love for them as displayed
in the Gospels (Matt 19:21; Mark 14:7; Luke 4:18, 14:12–14; John
12:8).

Racism toward African Americans in the eras of slavery and Jim
Crow created an underclass of people where poverty was undeniable.
At a time when many predominately white Christian denominations
and churches perpetuated racist ideologies such as the curse of "Ham
theory," supported racial segregation in every form of American life,
and forced Black Christians out of their churches, Black liberation
theology challenged the unbiblical practices of bigotry and racism.
In developing his early writings, Cone raises the question, "What has
the gospel of Jesus Christ to do with the Black struggle for justice in
the United States?"[20] The application of a Christ-centered, biblically

---

[18.] Cone, *For My People*, 40.

[19.] Joe R. Feagin, *Systemic Racism: A Theory of Oppression* (New York: Routledge, 2006), 2.

[20.] James Cone, *A Black Theology of Liberation, Twentieth Anniversary Edition* (Maryknoll, NY: Orbis, 1995), xi.

anchored, spirit-empowered, social crisis sermon, even today, challenges hearers to grapple with this question and other sinful realities that threaten to rob humanity of God's redemptive purposes.

My critique and concern about Cone's liberation theology argument is related to his deeply imbedded insistence that "there can be no theology of the gospel which does not arise from an oppressed community."[21] The revelation of God in Christ cannot be limited to oppressed communities. Cone's assertion arises from centering the Black experience in America as the defining concern of Christian theology. I argue that while any theology that has Christ at the center ought to encourage believers to "compassionately care for and radically confront social crises in the communities where their neighbors live, work, worship, and play," the depth and breadth of Christian theology encompasses more than the Black experience. Solid Christian theology is concerned with spiritual and social dynamics that both transcend and extend beyond any ethnicity in America. I disagree with Cone's epistemological argument that limits the revelation of God to afflicted and oppressed communities. Nevertheless, as I note in chapter 2, the church is best equipped to address social crises from the Word of God when we learn to appreciate the positive presuppositions held by biblically centered, interpretive communities.

Another critique of Cone's early theology is a flaw that Cone himself recognizes. He admits that a weakness in his argument in earlier editions of *A Black Theology of Liberation* was his interpretation of racism as "a domestic problem, largely associated with the exclusion of blacks from the benefits of American capitalism. Racism was primarily identified as a social exclusion with disastrous political and economic consequences."[22] Cone was correct in his assessment of the vices of racism on Black life in America, but he admits that the focus of his theology failed to encompass the totality and complexities of human oppression. Social crisis preaching acknowledges that sin, as separation from God, is the primary culprit of all social crisis. It brings the full weight of the gospel of Christ to bear on those complexities that were formerly excluded from Cone's theology.

Finally, I believe that Black liberation theology does not emphasize

---

21. Cone, 5.
22. Cone, xvii.

reconciliation enough. While liberation from social evil is a focus, reconciliation does not appear to receive the same enthusiasm. The Black liberation theologies of Albert Cleage, Cone, and Gayraud Wilmore, among others, do not extend to reconciliation as an earthly or eschatological mandate of the Bible. The New Testament is replete with God's plan to restore humanity into a right harmony with God and other human beings. Nowhere is that truth more prominent than Paul's teachings on ethnic unity and reconciliation in Christ: "That he might create in himself one new man in place of the two, so making peace, and might reconcile us both to God in one body through the cross, thereby killing the hostility" (Eph 2:15b–16 ESV).

On the other hand, J. Deotis Roberts, Black liberation theologian and contemporary of Cone, in his classic text *Liberation and Reconciliation*, insists that racial reconciliation should follow liberation. Roberts states, "Sin as moral evil, as it manifests itself in the brokenness in human relations (between blacks and whites), is personal and social. Blacks as well as whites must reckon with the personal and social directions of sin."[23] I am aware of the pros and cons of liberation theologies and insist that social crisis preaching confronts injustice, shows compassion for our neighbor, and maintains biblical fidelity. Just as the believer is involved in the lifelong process of spiritual sanctification, the process should also affect our social realities and relationship with God and humanity. This is the only evidence we have of the inner working of salvation and sanctification. The church cannot settle for liberated souls among terrorized bodies and communities.

TOWARDS A RATIONALE FOR SOCIAL CRISIS PREACHING

Proclamation is the most effective tool to address social injustice and social crisis from a Christian perspective, due to the transforming power of the Word of God proclaimed. In times of crises, proclamation, rather than political action, radically strikes at the root of social crises—and that root is sin. Political action, while necessary, often leaves sin unscathed and hidden. Proclamation seeks to transform

---

[23.] J. Deotis Roberts, *Liberation and Reconciliation*, 2nd ed. (Louisville: Westminster, 2005), 57.

hearts and lives while uncovering sin in its various manifestations. We need to hear and heed God's voice speaking to spiritual maladies and social madness. Preaching that does not show how the grand themes of the Bible, such as redemption, creation, salvation, the day of the Lord, and atonement, to name a few, are applicable to the social crises that affect image-bearers, misses the opportunity to invite hearers into the redemption narrative in tangible ways. Abstract sermons fail to connect these grand themes to the relevancy of people's hurts, fears, and concerns. Preachers must apprise their congregations of the spiritual and social conditions of their communities. God has spoken and is speaking. He is intimately concerned with the injustices in every community.

Some may contend that evangelistic preaching is the only kind the world needs. This approach, focusing merely on personal conversion, is a priority; but it is only an element of preaching, not the whole of it. It does not usually address how sinful individuals, living in a collective society comprised of institutions that operate in complex systems and structures, are often responsible for the brokenness of people and communities. The gospel must address the sin inherent in individuals and society for the church to realize the full manifestation of God's purpose for his creation. In other words, social crisis preaching does not simply aim at addressing the biblical or contemporary crises, but at theological truths that point to Christ. The rectification of the crises is not the *telos* of social crisis preaching, but rather it is Christ.

Likewise, social crisis preaching aims to speak into the human situations of image-bearers. Genesis 1:27 clearly affirms, "God created man in his own image, he created him in the image of God." This truth has profound implications, not limited or bound to geography, ethnicity, gender, or age. Being created in God's image anchors our identity in the Creator, and solidifies the unique truth that humans alone share this mark of distinction. For the purpose of this book, the theological concept of being made in the image of God influences our ethics and how we disciple congregations to love other image-bearers. As image-bearers ourselves, we are to care for and respect other image-bearers. Relationally, humanity was created to live in harmony with one another as worshipers of the triune God.

Sin has marred our identity as image-bearers, though it did not have the power to destroy it. God's creative design in us transcends sin's power, and we are redeemed through Jesus Christ, God's Son, who is the express likeness of God (John 14:9). Sin in its various forms disrupts the harmony that image-bearers were meant to share with God and with one another. There are spiritual and social ramifications to sin's disruptive nature. Social crisis preaching addresses every aspect of the image-bearer's life. Spirit-filled preachers, also image-bearers, are called to leverage the gospel of Jesus Christ, through proclamation, on the spiritual and social lives of fellow image-bearers.

Preaching "about" Social Crisis

There is a difference between preaching "about" (or "on" or "around") a social issue and preaching "to" social crises. Preaching "about" social issues is an easy escape for the preacher who feels the burden to address the crisis but lacks the courage to confront the complicity to communal crises in the pews. You can provide data and related information about social issues and those that evolve into crises and still not address the injustices. Preaching about social crisis addresses the symptoms the congregation is comfortable condoning but can fail to address the root causes, of which we are often a part. We can preach about a social crisis and yet not provide the congregation with specific, meaningful, practical applications to tackle the injustices that every day affect the people we are called to love and serve. All it takes is for the preacher to skim the surface of the text, sprinkle in some news headlines, affirm God's love, and give the benediction.

Preaching about social issues does little to challenge biblical illiteracy and ministry complacency, nor does it make congregants more aware of the plight of the people across town. Preaching about social crises does little to adjust the scales of pulpits light on communal justice and heavy on the finer points of theology and personal piety. Communal justice and personal piety are tethered together, inseparable and indissoluble when joined together in proclamation. Preaching about social crises avoids cross-bearing, self-denial, and the marks of discipleship to which Jesus calls the preacher and hearer. Preaching about social crises leaves many parishioners asking, "Now what?" or "So what?"

Preaching "to" Social Crisis

Preaching "to" social crisis is the hard work of leading the church to become what Sally Brown calls "agents of redemptive interruption."[24] Preaching to social crisis is about more than providing information, remaining neutral, or affirming long-held, but false, assumptions and stereotypes about "the other." Preaching to social crisis involves digging deep into the text, finding the social tensions that the text addresses, naming them, shedding light on the contemporary parallels, delivering decisive application, then trusting God with the results. Preaching to social crisis moves congregations beyond fear and bigotry to new, refreshing, and redemptive spaces where they are compelled to extend the radical mercy of God. Preaching to social crisis helps the church members realize that they have been recipients of radical mercy. Preaching to social crisis goes beyond transferring information to the depths of experiencing the Christian faith. Brown also states

> Christian faith is not a cerebral affair – a matter of privately cherishing a specific set of religious beliefs. It is a shared way of life, a way of being fully human in company with others, and a way of deeply engaging the world that God so fiercely loves. We maintain relationship with the "other" we encounter within the Christian community, where tensions inevitably arise. . . . In Christ's name and with Christ's servant-like posture, we commit ourselves to support the well-being of the racially, ethnically, culturally, economically, and theologically different "other."[25]

In *The Responsible Pulpit*, James Earl Massey lists five components of the African American preaching tradition that "help any preacher from any tradition to sense more clearly how to keep the verbal witness of the pulpit both virile, engaging, and effective."[26] The five sermonic components are functional, festive, communal, radical, and climactic. Traces of each component may exist in social crisis

---

[24.] Sally A. Brown, *Sunday's Sermon for Monday's World: Preaching to Shape Daring Witness* (Grand Rapids: Eerdmans, 2020), xviii.

[25.] Brown, 23–24.

[26.] James Earl Massey, *The Responsible Pulpit* (Anderson, IN: Warner, 1974), chap. 6, Kindle.

preaching, but the most consistent and effective in social crisis preaching is the "radical" component. Historically, radicality has been the
most critical and constructive response to racism from the Black
church. Courageous social crisis preaching confronts sin everywhere.
Massey contends, "Radicality in the sermon engages the hearer. It
makes him know that he is being confronted, that necessity is being
laid upon him to respond. True preaching is always confrontational."[27]
Social crisis preaching is not an eloquent diatribe that simply identifies problems and introduces solutions. On the contrary, it demands
that the hearer break from any and all political, racial, economic,
or theological loyalties complicit in social crises. Luther D. Ivory
notes, "A critical prophetic voice must be accompanied by confrontational prophetic action."[28] Just as the nerves in our body alert us
to confront the serious illnesses lurking in our organs, social crisis
preaching takes prophetic action to confront the pain caused by the
sin of social injustice.

THE METHODOLOGY OF SOCIAL CRISIS PREACHING

In a world where we measure pastoral effectiveness by our number of
social media followers and church members, the social crisis preacher
is a fellow traveler who lives among and suffers "with" the people in
the pews. The methodology of social crisis preaching entails an incarnational model and an intentional homiletical approach. Pastors
commit themselves to be with the congregation, developing them to
intentionally care about and confront the crises in their neighbor's
communities.

Smith, Sr. in his book *Social Crisis Preaching*, refers to this as the
"pre-proclamation function of the preacher."[29] Pre-proclamation is
Smith Sr.'s first step in his delivery of the social crisis sermon. Smith
Sr. argues that the social crisis sermon begins before a word is uttered
from the pulpit, or even before the pen touches the paper in sermon or

---

27. Massey, chap. 6.
28. Luther D. Ivory, *Toward a Theology of Radical Involvement: The Theological Legacy of Martin Luther King, Jr.* (Nashville: Abingdon, 1997), 90.
29. Smith, Sr., *Social Crisis Preaching*, 80–81.

manuscript preparation. Pastors must enter into spaces where they can discuss hard, sensitive topics with their members. These conversations may take place en route to county school board meetings, deacons' meetings, over a latte at Starbucks, in hospital waiting rooms, over chili dogs while watching a playoff game, while driving to a party, or in the gym. No matter the venue, God opens the door for the pre-proclamation function. God opens the door for the pre-proclamation function of social crisis preaching. Pastors must be intentional, proactive, and seize these moments of discipleship. Pre-proclamation involves listening and hearing people's fears then leading them into redemptive truths from the Word of God. Irrational defenses, fears, and biases are more likely to be broken down in one-on-one conversations than they are in the company of the masses, where too often groupthink about a particular social issue overrides an individual's personal convictions and desire to enter into inclusive dialogue. The pre-proclamation function of the preacher is perhaps the most important factor in social crisis preaching. It is incarnational in that it requires the preacher's involvement and engagement with the people to whom they will be preaching. Pre-proclamation also calls the preacher to be informed about social crises. Congregations are more accepting and less critical of preachers who are knowledgeable about the crises being addressed, who have been with them as they live through them, rather than someone disengaged and unfamiliar with their issues.

Ezekiel sitting "with" the exiles in Tel Aviv illustrates this model. In holy resignation, he utters, "I sat where they sat." (Ezek 3:15b KJV). Moses exemplifies this as he "chose to suffer with the people of God rather than to enjoy the fleeting pleasure of sin" (Heb 11:25; Exod 2:10–12). Paul is the creative exemplar of the social crisis preacher, renouncing his privilege and position. In his letter to the church at Philippi, he writes, "I am persuaded of this, I know that I will remain and continue with all of you for your progress and joy in the faith" (Phil 1:25). Chief and paramount is the incarnate second person of the Trinity, Jesus Christ, engaged in *kenosis* (Phil 2:7), self-emptying, to dwell among us (John 1:14) fallen humans, those he came to save and deliver. Effective social crisis preaching is the result of preacher and congregation having a heart for the poor, disenfranchised, overlooked, rejected, and forgotten. Jesus models pastoral compassion and advocacy in the Gospels by demonstrating how he spent his life pursuing and serving those who were in crises situations.

I receive questions from my students and other pastors such as, "How do you do social crisis preaching?" and "Is social crisis preaching a different or special kind of preaching?" The first methodological question will be treated in detail in Part 2. The answer to the second is both "no" and "yes." It lies in a methodological model that views expository and topical preaching as the homiletical approach to engage in social crisis preaching that "drives congregations to compassionately care for and radically confront social crises in the communities where their neighbors live, work, worship, and play."

Social Crisis Preaching Is Expository Preaching

Is social crisis preaching a special kind of preaching? No, in that all Scripture was written in a context where spiritual crises inevitably caused social crises. In this way, we see social crisis preaching as not simply a duty to perform on the periodic occasion when breaking news floods the headlines, but as a constant response to our awareness of the plight of our neighbor. Social crisis preaching is performed out of an overflow of love for all our neighbors, not just those who have social crises with which we are most familiar. The foundation of all social crisis preaching is love for people and the unquenchable quest to see them freed from the mind-numbing, restrictive situations in which they perpetually find themselves. We do this by the power of God's grace "to rescue us from this present evil age, according to the will of our God and Father" (Gal 1:4b).

One model of social crisis preaching is expository preaching, a proclamation of what the text says. The late E.K. Bailey said, "Expository preaching [is] a message that focuses on a specific portion of Scripture, so as to clearly establish the precise meaning of the text, and to poignantly motivate the hearers to actions or attitudes dictated by that text in the power of the Holy Spirit."[30] Expository preaching should be appraised on the sermon's ability to produce applicable points and

---

[30.] Robert Smith Jr., *Doctrine That Dances: Bringing Doctrinal Preaching and Teaching to Life* (Nashville: B&H, 2008), 19–20.

principles. The preacher who engages in sound exegetical practices will lead hearers to direct, specific application from the texts. The specific application will lead the hearer to engage and encounter other human beings in their complex social world. The correct application of God's Word leads to a biblical worldview and behaviors that manifest themselves in relationships, activities, practices, and commitments that are, at least in part, social. Preaching that does not address our contemporary situations is merely an exercise in biblical exegesis and explanation. These pastors are not being faithful representatives and mouthpieces of God. The parishioner comes to church to hear, "Thus saith the Lord," and is asking the question, "What does God have to say about this social crisis event that took place this weekend?"

The pastor must tend the flock. Thomas G. Long contends, "It would be a mistake, however, to make too sharp a distinction between 'pastoral' and 'prophetic' sermons, as if personal issues could be separated from their placement in the social context and vice versa."[31] To not engage in contemporary situations is to lead your flock to a pasture with dead grass and a lake with no water. Sin not only disrupts our relationship with God (Gen 3:8–11, 23–24), but also with one another (Gen 3:16–19). The depths of sin's effect on the social order is clearly seen when Adam and Eve's son Cain murdered his brother Abel (Gen 4:8). Sin infiltrates the social order where humanity exists. Don't believe me? Turn on the evening news. Sin corrupts the institutions we construct and maintain (Mark 11:15–18) and seeps into the political, social, and civic world that the body of Christ inhabits. Thus, social crisis preaching is inescapable if we preach the Scriptures with exegetical, hermeneutical, and homiletical integrity.

How do we preach Luke 12:13–21, the parable of the rich fool, without confronting corporate greed and economic exploitation, bringing it face-to-face with employees on strike or assembly line workers without healthcare benefits? A pastor provides the congregational application to Eph 2:14 by confronting local racial hostility and challenging the congregation to actively pursue peace through sacrificial actions in the same way Christ did. Long further comments, "The gospel does not

---

31. Thomas G. Long, *The Witness of Preaching* (Louisville: Westminster/John Knox, 1989), 242.

speak to isolated individuals and then swivel to speak another word to the world of politics and social systems. The Bible speaks to the totality of human life."[32] Whether you preach through the liturgical calendar or preach systematically through the books of the Bible, you will have to deal with the social crises in the biblical text and the ones affecting the people in the pews.

Social Crisis Preaching Is Topical Preaching

Social crisis preaching requires strategy and methodology to address the pressing issues on the hearts of God's people. Preachers must meet people where they are and lead them to where God desires them to be, by the Word of God. Topical preaching, done responsibly, allows preachers to consider hot, sensitive, and growing local issues from the Bible. Concerning topical preaching, Robert Smith, Jr. rightly contends

> Texts have to speak to people in their own *Sitz im Leben* (situation in life). Preaching that addresses only the what question of the implications of the text without responding to the *so what* question of the application of the text to daily concerns and vice versa is neither authentically expository nor responsibly topical. Responsible topical preaching can serve as a bridge for the kind of topical preaching that has been guilty of searching newspaper articles and television shows for relevant and timely topics without adequately treating the text and the type of peaching that masquerades as expository preaching without sufficiently addressing the human plight.[33]

Is social crisis preaching a special kind of preaching? Yes. And it is also a special kind of sermon. A topical sermon will allow the preacher to responsibly address significant social crises moments when they arise. Though we must not confine social crisis preaching to the headline-making events (police abuse of force, rising pandemic death counts,

---

[32.] Long, 242.

[33.] Robert Smith Jr., "Topical," in *The New Interpreters Handbook of Preaching*, ed. Paul Scott Wilson (Nashville: Abingdon, 2008), 425.

executive orders that disrupt and displace communities, unprecedented rise in gun-related murders, terrorist attacks), nor should we shy away from headlines. Why? Because the people of God are often the headlines. God's people need to hear a word from the Lord concerning the headlines that affect their lives and the people they love. Social crisis preaching, then, is a word, "in season and out of season" (2 Tim 4:2).

Historical moments like the Civil War, the Civil Rights Movement, and current situations like the mounting tension surrounding civil unions, beckon the preacher to turn to the Bible and tune in to the social world around them and their parishioners. Smith further concludes, "Jesus preached the truth of God's Word as he encountered the topical and thematic contexts of his hearers."[34] These special moments require heralds of the gospel to pivot to a topical social crisis sermon that addresses and provides biblical direction and hope for the people in the pews most affected by those situations. Is it irresponsible of the pastor to be aware of the fears that trouble the minds of most people, only to remain mute? Yes! Is it irresponsible to stay silent while conversations about these fears occur in almost every space of society—social media, the classroom, workplace, barbershops, boardrooms, and newsrooms—except the pulpit? Yes! Where else will God's truth and justice be proclaimed? Where else will our parishioners and community find visions of justice, glimpses of hope, and gestures of mercy? Certain newsworthy and community-shaking events demand preachers prepare a sermon to deal with the thoughts and concerns of their parishioners. Whether through expository preaching or responsible topical preaching, pastors must preach through the power of the Holy Spirit to "develop and drive congregations to compassionately care for and radically confront social crises in the communities where their neighbors live, work, worship, and play."

Conclusion

Many of the ancient biblical crises have a corresponding parallel today. In the Bible, "times of social upheaval and stress"[35] may refer to slavery

---

[34.] Smith Jr., 426.
[35.] Smith Sr., *Social Crisis Preaching*, 18.

in Egypt (Exod 1:8–14), the devaluing of human life in the worship of Molech (2 Kgs 23:10), genocide (Esth 3), food deprivation (Ruth 1; John 6:1–7), massive health crises (Matt 15:29–31), ethical bias (Acts 10; Gal 2), or forms of greed (Josh 7; Luke 12:16–21; Acts 5; James 5:1–6). Social crises result from the spiritual crisis of sin, both individual and structural. Sex trafficking and sex slavery, poverty, abortion, rampant crime rates, human trafficking, racism, social injustice, and family dysfunction are the social byproducts of individual and structural sin stemming from the fall. Such crises reflect our contemporary "times of upheaval and stress." Bryan Chapell would argue that contemporary believers share a mutual human condition with those for whom or by whom the text was written.[36] Quite often, this shared human condition is the product of a particular social crisis.

Throughout history, those dedicated to changing the social order have advanced human progress, against those committed to maintaining the status quo. Consider Martin Luther's response to the Catholic Church's corruption, over and against those who attempted to silence and malign him. His commitment and fidelity to Scripture produced spiritual and social change within the church. When dark forces sought to maintain and perpetuate the evil institution of slavery that had already lasted 247 years, the preaching responses of Frederick Douglass and William Lloyd Garrison set the process of human freedom in motion.

In the years following the Civil War, the prophetic proclamation of Daniel Payne and Henry McNeal Turner was a bastion of resistance against lynching and government-sponsored disenfranchisement against Blacks. Responding to the dehumanizing realities and emotionally destructive ordeals of the Jim Crow era, Martin Luther King, Jr., Adam Clayton Powell, Sr., Fred Shuttlesworth, Reverdy Cassius Ransom, and countless others advanced America to a new era of human progress and hope. Leading the charge in almost every period of social change were preachers committed to the principles of social crisis preaching.

[36.] See Bryan Chapell, "Fallen Condition Focus" in *Christ Centered Preaching: Redeeming the Expository Sermon, 2nd ed.* (Grand Rapids: Baker, 2005).

CHAPTER 1:

CUES AND CLUES

Finding the Social Crisis in the Text

Since the fall (Gen 3; Rom 5:12), humanity has been in a constant state of social crisis. God has given us his written Word that recounts to us the world in which social crises played out. The biblical authors' milieus denoted contexts in which imperial domination, economic exploitation, and religious corruption were the order of the day. Thus, to relegate the teachings of Scripture and the message of salvation to an entirely spiritual consequence—devoid of social impact—is to ignore the immediate reaches of the Word of God in the realms of the social world in which the Word came to serve. The Bible provides the principles and ethics to deal with our contemporary social crises, because the biblical writers wrote amid social crises. Why do some preachers find it difficult to move from the Scriptures to address current social issues in their sermons without feeling like they are imposing on the text? Since social crisis preaching is "biblically rooted, Spirit-enabled proclamation that develops and drives congregations to compassionately care for and radically confront social crises in the communities where their neighbors live, work, worship, and play," pastors carry out the discipleship mandates of the Bible through the pastoral calling of preaching.

This chapter will ensure that the preacher is equipped to address social crises from the Bible, and to do so with integrity and confidence. The objection that preachers cannot find applicable text to address current social crises in their communities is not a valid reason to avoid preaching on social and political issues. Because social crises affect people in our pews, to not shepherd people in crises is irrespon-sible. This preaching is motivated by the love we have for them. It is incumbent on the preacher, as "sacred anthropologist," to bring the Word of God to bear on the social crises in our time. If one contends that politics, social matters, or civic concerns are not the concerns of the pulpit, you need this chapter. There is no realm under heaven and earth where God does not have dominion or where his Word is lacking in authority.

Additionally, this chapter will cover hermeneutical and exegetical approaches to social crisis preaching. I will provide four cues and clues to help preachers engage in social crisis preaching from Scripture by identifying five areas of location in the text to address the social crises in our times: (1) shifts in emphasis of the biblical author, (2) exegetical insights, (3) biblical themes, (4) storytelling and narrative preaching, and (5) the world in front of the text.

Again, the source of all social crisis preaching is the Bible. Social crisis preaching does not permit preachers to cherry-pick Scripture verses to support a political or social agenda, nor does it aim at Band-Aid solutions to resolve social crises. Instead, social crisis preaching intends to be exact in presenting biblical solutions to social crises. Preaching to social issues, like any form of preaching, requires the preacher to commit to solid exegetical analysis of the text, interpret-ing the text in its context, then finding the big idea of the text—with the aid of the Holy Spirit. Social crisis preaching does not dismiss the theology of the text nor jettison the preaching text after it is read, in favor of providing commentary on some political or social issue. Smith Sr. insists that social crisis preachers ask, "Does the idea of the preacher harmonize with the Word of God or is it simply an echo of the voice of society?"[1]

THE AUTHOR'S SHIFT IN EMPHASIS

As a young recruit in the United States Navy, the first lesson I learned was attention to detail. Later, when I was assigned to my ship, the

[1.] Smith, Sr., *Social Crisis Preaching*, 82 (see intro., n. 10).

U.S.S. Saratoga (CV-60), during the Operation Desert Shield/Desert Storm conflict, I further learned that, in some situations, attention to detail—or not—could be a matter of life and death. The narratives in Scripture are replete with details. The preacher is responsible for getting the details right. Failing to do so could lead to disastrous outcomes and missed opportunities to address social crises. The shifting emphases in the narratives do not mean there is a contradiction in thought or a different meaning the author seeks to convey. Instead, the details provide the reader with differences in insight, greater clarity to the thrust and application of the text, and the flexibility for the preacher to further emphasize a specific detail in one narrative that may not be apparent in another.

The Emphases of the Evangelists in the Gospels

A biblical author's shifting emphasis is most evident in the Gospel accounts. Each Gospel writer has a different audience and focus. They communicate four unique but authoritative accounts of the life of Jesus. Yet, in some instances, even when the events are similar, the details are different. The author could further highlight a particular word or phrase for the sake of emphasis. Let us take the Beatitudes, for example. In Matthew's Gospel, they are referred to as "The Sermon on the Mount" (Matt 5:3–12), while the Gospel of Luke contains a similar, yet shorter group of teachings, referred to as "The Sermon on the Plain" (Luke 6:20–49). Kenneth E. Bailey addresses one significant emphasis:

> In both passages a Christological affirmation appears in the center of the "sandwich." One difference is that in Luke there are seven words/phrases in the center while in Matthew the entire Beatitude forms a "sandwich" of seven phrases. These sandwiches give the topic of persecution a singular and significant emphasis.[2]

In Luke 6:20, Luke uses πτωχός, translated "who are poor," to emphasize one who is bereft of material possessions, a beggar, or someone

---

[2] Kenneth E. Bailey, *Jesus Through Middle Eastern Eyes: Cultural Studies in the Gospels* (Downers Grove, IL: InterVarsity, 2008), 66.

dependent on others for support. On the other hand, Matthew uses the phrase πτωχοί τω πνεύματι, translated "poor in spirit." According to Justo L. González, Luke will not "allow us to avoid the poignancy of these blessings and woes by spiritualizing them, as does Matthew."[3] While this does not suggest a contradiction in the meaning of the Beatitudes, it does allow the preacher to interpret the meaning of the text within its context, while highlighting specific emphases that speak to a social crisis, both in the text and in the preacher's social context. González describes the thrust of Luke's Gospel as, "good news to the poor and the powerless. It is also good news to the rich and the mighty, but only if they follow a path of radical obedience, which in turn will affect their riches and their power."[4]

I believe responsible social crisis preaching will not pit one Gospel and its emphasis on the spiritually poor against the other Gospel, with its emphasis on the earthly or materially poor, nor ignore one for the other. Preaching our example texts, with their shifting emphases, mandates the social crisis preacher to find the locus of meaning in the life of Jesus, while also borrowing this saying from the prophet Isaiah, who proclaims the kingdom for the poor (Isa 66:2). The preacher who selects either of these texts should not merely spiritualize the sayings of Jesus by disconnecting them from how Luke's socially and economically poor would have heard them, having read Isaiah. Therefore, the preacher can apply the gospel to the social context of the contemporary poor by challenging the congregation to care about and confront the social crises in their neighbor's community. This text in the Beatitudes from Luke's Gospel requires the preacher to allow Jesus's teaching to speak to the social concerns of the poor, both in Luke's audience and in the preacher's congregation. Such application cannot be avoided, even when a preacher selects a similar pericope from the Gospel of Matthew.

Similarly, when the social crisis preacher, as an interpreter of the Word of God, considers the audience, along with the cultural and historical background within each Gospel, they should leverage the emphasis of each Gospel account to address the social crisis in a manner that keeps with the themes and nuances of that particular account. For instance,

---

[3.] Justo L. González, *Luke, A Theological Commentary on the Bible*, (Louisville: Westminster/John Knox, 2010), 93.

[4.] González, *Luke*, 93.

Matthew is written to influence a Jewish audience of the Messianic claims of Jesus as the son of David. Yet, there are clues and cues within that Gospel that communicate that, from the lineage of Jesus, other nations are an integral part of God's story of redemption. What might this say to communities who assume a position of ethnic or cultural superiority? Using the cultural and historical background of this Gospel, how can the preacher encourage those who feel excluded as ethnic minorities in the church, workplace, and the community? What does such information say to how we view women? The preacher must keep this historical and cultural context in mind, because these facts play a significant role in how the pericopes in the Gospel of Matthew are interpreted.

In Luke, there is a very prominent theme of Jesus's preferential treatment of the poor and despised, and his rebuke of the rich (Luke 6:24–26). Jesus is born to poor parents (Luke 2:1–7), who are met by shepherds in the birth narrative (Luke 2:8–20), not by kings as in the Gospel of Matthew (Matt 2:1–12). Jesus's message in the synagogue is good news to poor people (Luke 4:18–19). In Luke 7:22, Jesus enthusiastically bellows to the messengers of John his social crisis ministry to the poor by proclaiming, "Go and report to John what you have seen and heard: The blind receive their sight, the lame walk, those with leprosy are cleansed, the deaf hear, the dead are raised, and the poor are told the good news."

Both the presence and message of Jesus are in strong resistance to the spiritual, socioeconomic, and political forces that make people sightless, immobile, ostracized, disabled, and poor. The cue and clue for social crisis preachers in the Gospel of Luke are the ministry and message of Jesus, as emphasized by the evangelist. The social crisis preacher is required to move in the direction of the Gospel writer. In Luke's account of the "Sermon on the Plain," it is no mistake that he includes the "woes" to the rich and powerful (Luke 6:24–26), whereas in the Gospel of Matthew, these rebukes are not present.

Shifting Emphasis in the Old Testament Narrative: The Bronze Snake

Another example of shifting emphasis is the difference of stress placed on the bronze serpent in Numbers 21 and 2 Kings 18. The latter is a powerful exposition on how the sacred can quickly become profane and idolatrous. In Numbers 21, God commands his people to make the bronze serpent (Num 21:8–9). The serpent is also meant to point beyond itself to something greater, namely Yahweh's power over the serpent. But by 2 Kings 18, the same bronze serpent, created for a sacred purpose, becomes the focus of idolatry. There is a shift in emphasis "from" the bronze serpent as a symbol that points to God (Num 21:9) "to" a relic that "the Israelites were burning incense to . . . ." (2 Kgs 18:4).

In Numbers 21, there is a social (and spiritual) crisis. The people, en route to freedom, encounter hunger and thirst in the wilderness. After complaining, poisonous serpents bite the Israelites to their death. For their healing, a countermeasure is put in place. Moses, the deliverer, is instructed by Yahweh to make a bronze serpent and set it on a pole (Num 21:8–9). Those bitten were instructed to gaze up at the snake, for the snake is a reminder of their crisis, as well as a sign of Yahweh's triumph over it. The bronze serpent, comments David L. Stubbs, "is more than a sign of judgment. It is also a sign of God's victory over the serpent. Like the head of an enemy placed on the tip of a spear and shown to the people."[5]

A social crisis sermon focused on Numbers 21 and 2 Kings 18 can address idolatry and misplaced affections and how they damage social and human relationships. In the case of the bronze serpent in Numbers 21, 800 years later, the object that directed the people to Yahweh became a rival for his worship. The bronze serpent was constructed by Moses and preserved until the days of Hezekiah; the people of Israel had been making offerings to it (2 Kgs 18:4). The first commandment strictly forbids the worship of anything but Yahweh.

Application: Idolatry of Wealth

This shift in emphasis between the two narratives in Numbers 21 and 2 Kings 18 is the cue and clue that allow the social crisis preacher to address one of the main culprits of social injustice: idolatry. Once

---

[5.] David L. Stubbs, *Numbers*, Brazos Theological Commentary on the Bible (Grand Rapids: Brazos, 2009), 169.

the sermon defines the sin of idolatry and identifies it in 2 Kings 18, it lays the foundation for specific applications to the contemporary audience by dealing with the various forms of idolatry at the root of contemporary social crises, and why they need to be crushed, just like the bronze snake. For this sermon, the preacher may consider naming the idolatry of money or wealth. Like Moses's bronze snake, money and wealth should be used for God-glorifying purposes (Prov 22:9; 29:7; Matt 6:2–4; Acts 2:44–46; Gal 2:10; 1 Tim 6:17–18; Heb 13:16), but over time, it can become the bronze snake that we idolize and worship.

When we idolize material wealth, there is the propensity for the sin of greed. Greed leads to economic exploitation of vulnerable people (Prov 13:11; 14:31; 22:16; 28:25) that manifests in the everyday realities that cripple and crush poor communities: hunger, minimum wage jobs, unsafe working conditions, predatory lending, payday loan companies, lack of health insurance, and perhaps most heinous of all, the inability to build wealth and pass it to the next generation.

Application: Misplaced Affections

The social crisis preacher can also identify specific congregational idols that can serve as points of application. Long contends, "The word of God we encounter in Scripture does not attack idolatry in general; it dethrones our idols, severs the bonds of our old and crippling loyalties."[6] This text can also speak to the idolatry of worship itself or false worship. Amos speaks to this sin when he says

> I hate, I despise, your feasts! I can't stand the stench of your solemn assemblies. Even if you offer me your burnt offerings and grain offerings, I will not accept them; I have no regard for your fellowship offerings of fattened cattle. Take away from me the noise of your songs! I will not listen to the music of your harps. (Amos 5:21–23)

Our dead, misplaced affections can be the source of idolatry, rendering our spiritual barometer ineffective in registering the mounting

---

[6.] Thomas G. Long, *The Witness of Preaching* (Louisville: Westminster/John Knox, 1989), 55.

pressures of a cold, heartless world. Whenever the spiritual vitality of the church wanes, social crises emerge and rise. For instance, advances of the civil rights era and our love for our country, both originally intended to lift and lead people out of despair into the promise of hope, have become objects of misplaced loyalty and affection.

Misplaced Affection in Idols of the Past

Many African American churches have gone from being Spirit-inspired participants in God's movement for justice, to immobile spectators amused with religious monuments and museums. Eddie Glaude, Jr.'s analysis is accurate: ". . . such a church loses its power. Memory becomes its currency. Its soul withers from neglect. The result is all too often church services and liturgies that entertain, but lack a spirit that transforms, and preachers who deign for followers instead of fellow travelers in God."[7]

Many African American congregations glory in the prizes, personalities, and period of freedom, rather than the God who gave us freedom! The faithful prophetic proclamation from the Black pulpit that once stirred the nation's conscience has given way to prosperity preaching that blends extreme capitalism with excessive individualism. That which once pointed people to the God of justice, advocated for human agency, and led humans of every hue to recognize one another as image-bearers, years later has demanded offerings in exchange for the elusive quest for the prosperity of health and wealth.

Misplaced Affections in Idolatry of Nation

On a recent grocery-store run, an image caught my eye that would generally have gone unnoticed by me, and most likely, the hundreds of motorists traveling that stretch of highway. The image goes unnoticed because it is normal, acceptable, fits the values and mores of our citizenry, and receives very little pushback or resistance. That image exists in a churchyard. Two flags atop a flagpole. The stars and stripes

---

7. Eddie Glaude, Jr. "The Black Church is Dead," *HuffPost,* August 23, 2021, https://www.huffpost.com/entry/the-black-church-is-dead_b_473815.

above the Christian flag. That day, that image reminded me of our controversial and conflicting identities as Christians and Americans. For some people, the two are synonymous.

Consider how 2 Kings 18 speaks to this reality. The goddess Asherah was known for her association with serpents. The bronze snake that Moses made must have started to become indistinguishable from the snakes that represented the goddess Asherah. Just as "Nehushtan" (2 Kgs 18:4) sounds like the Hebrew word for both bronze and serpent, and just as the bronze serpent Moses made became associated with the serpents of the goddess Asherah, for some, "Christian" and "American" can become indistinguishable. This is idolatry. Yet it is common to find expressions of patriotism in Christian worship and to fall prey to nationalistic forms of Christianity.

As Christians who love America, there are moments when our nation's goals, vision, and values, and the Kingdom of God are antithetical. As Christians, we must realize that when the two conflict, "we must obey God, rather than men" (Acts 5:29 ESV). Although it is possible for Christians to salute and honor the bravery of women and men who sacrificed for our country, we must give our highest and unwavering allegiance to the sacrificial Lamb of God, who gives us true liberty. The Constitution and the Bible are not the same. Caesar and Christ are not equal. And the flag is not comparable to the cross, no matter how much they seem the same.

EXEGETICAL INSIGHTS

The time and preparation involved in the exegetical study is invaluable to preaching. In fact, word studies that attempt to determine a word's contextual meaning can add significant social crisis insights to biblical texts read and translated in English. These exegetical insights that the preacher gains through word studies, exegetical analysis, and cultural investigation allow them to bridge the gap between the biblical and the present world.

Exegetical insights also provide new pathways for preachers to usher congregations, traditionally reluctant to address social issues, to tackle the mounting social crises that bombard our social media and news feeds. Every preacher should pray for the Holy Spirit to provide pinpoint accuracy, error-free precision, and detailed exposition so that believers "may be filled with the knowledge of his will in all wisdom and spiritual understanding, so that you may walk worthy of the Lord, fully pleasing to him: bearing fruit in every good work and growing in the knowledge of God" (Col 1:9–10).

The most precise and biblically sound way to address social crises from the Bible is by embracing a grammatical-historical literary hermeneutic and using the exegetical tools accompanying that approach. Words open the door through which we walk our congregations through the meaning of the text into what it is saying to us. When we fail to investigate the meaning of words and how they were used in their original contexts, we forfeit the valuable insights necessary to clearly and precisely interpret the text. Some of these words are significant for social crisis preaching. Words can provide valuable cues and clues to help the preacher move seamlessly, and with integrity, to address social issues in sermonic form.

Righteousness and Justice: A Wider View

The word *justice* is sparsely seen in the English translation of the New Testament. Steven Voth offers an alarming study:

> A computer search for the word "justice" in the KJV finds that "justice" appears only 28 times in the entire Bible. A further interesting fact is that of those 28 uses of the term justice, none are to be found in the New Testament translation of the KJV. All 28 occurrences of this English word appear in the Old Testament. To express this another way, people who during their entire lifetime read the New Testament of the KJV would have never come across the word "justice" in their reading . . . . The same search carried out in the RVR reveals that the word "justicia" (justice) appears a total of 370 times. The term can be found 101 times in the New Testament.[8]

[8.] Steven Voth, "Justice vs. Righteousness: A Contextualized Analysis of 'tsedeq' in the KJV (English) and RVR (Spanish)," in *The Challenge of Bible Translation: Communicating God's Word to*

One must examine how this translation decision influences some of the church's erroneous theology and social and political positions during the seventeenth through the mid-twentieth centuries, when the most familiar Bible on nightstands, coffee tables, and large oak pulpits was the King James Version. Although modern English translations have improved on this issue, this translation problem continues to concern some preachers and biblical scholars. While I do not wish to argue for or against a particular translation, my aim is to promote a more thorough exegetical study and stir our consciences to ask why we don't read about justice as frequently in New Testament text, except as it relates to individual salvific topics.

In the Old Testament, the Hebrew word for justice is *mishpat*. Often in the Old Testament *mishpat* (justice) is paired with *tsedeqa* (righteousness) (2 Sam 8:15; 2 Chr 9:8; Ps 89:14; Isa 33:5; Amos 5:7; 5:24). I wish to convey for this discussion how the communal and corporate aspects of *tsedeq* and *misphat* need to be reestablished, when appropriate, through careful and responsible exegetical analysis to address the social crisis through Christian preaching. Likewise, when we miss this exegetical insight, by focusing entirely on personal piety, personal purity and holiness, and individual morality, we will dull the expectancy of congregations to hold their ecclesiastical and political leaders accountable, by ensuring that they make justice an integral component of their administrative practices and policies. Lastly, when we dig beneath the surface of the English translations of the Bible and into the core of the various nuances of the word *tsedeq*, we can draw special attention to God as one who loves and requires social justice, specifically for the poor person and outcast.

Voth recommends, "There are many contexts in which the best rendition of *tsedeq* is achieved through the word or concept 'justice.' This is especially true when *tsedeq* is used in parallelism with *mispat*."[9] Identifying these passages provides an exegetical insight as a clue into how the preacher can move from text to sermon to communicate God's expectation of justice, and our response to injustice. If social crisis preachers are not aware of the nuances of this word during sermon

---

the World, ed. Glen G. Scorgie, Mark L. Strauss, and Steven M. Voth (Grand Rapids: Zondervan, 2003), 282.
    9. Voth, 288.

preparation, they will forfeit any opportunity to properly disciple congregations to become seekers of justice for their neighbors.

This translation issue, well-known to Hebrew Bible and New Testament scholars, has not only led to significant exegetical insights in New Testament passages that contain the words "righteous," "righteousness," and "justice," but it shines a light on the reason why justice is not proclaimed from more pulpits. In the New Testament, informs Nicholas Wolterstorff, "The great bulk of *dik*-stem words are translated with grammatical variants on our word 'right.' The noun, for example, is usually translated 'righteousness,' not as 'justice.'"[10] Knowing when a passage is better translated as "justice" instead of "righteousness" can determine to what extent we require congregations to challenge systemic injustices, derivative of personal morality. This is why preachers must go beyond dependency on their favorite biblical translation. Wolsterstorff notes, "Unless the notion of legal judgment is so prominent in the context as virtually to force a translation in terms of justice, the translators will prefer to speak of righteousness."[11] Social crisis preaching will balance personal responsibility with corporate responsibility; how we translate and interpret the "righteousness" and "justice" passages will determine if a congregation embraces an imbalanced theology.

For some, unless there is a deep dive into exegetical studies, they simply don't see frequent occurrences of the word justice; therefore, personal piety becomes the primary and overarching theme of the New Testament and the aim of all preaching. The decisions facing translators, dating back to the Septuagint translation of the Hebrew Bible to Greek, on where to translate *tsedeqa* and *mishpat* in the New Testament as "justice," was and continues to be a daunting task. To be clear, the semantic range of *tsedaqa* is expansive; using one English word to define those wide ranges of meaning is almost impossible. Sound exegesis dictates that context should be the primary determining factor in the precise meaning of words that share the same or similar stems or roots.

In Isaiah 40–55, the righteousness of Yahweh reflects his salvation and deliverance for His covenant community. Voth contends, "In the Psalms, God's *tsedeq* comes to the aid of cities, the oppressed, the

---

10. Nicholas Wolterstorff, *Justice: Rights and Wrongs* (Princeton, NJ: Princeton University, 2008), 111.
11. Wolterstorff, 113.

abandoned, the afflicted, etc. This intervention of God on behalf of the ones in need is expressed through the word *tsedeq*."[12] Both *tsedeq* and *misphat* have meanings beyond what is expressed through our English word *righteousness*, which almost always means "right moral conduct" or "an individual's right standing before God." While an individual's right moral conduct is vital, if not the primary fruit of Christian salvation, social crisis preachers must also show how individuals influence institutions and how the justice and righteousness of God speak to both.

THEMES AND DOCTRINES THROUGHOUT THE BIBLE

Christians love, worship, and serve God in Christ, because God has revealed in his Word and in his Son, his love, care, and concern for humanity through his willingness to be in relationship with us. Therefore, preaching themes and doctrines should reveal God's love, care, and concern for humanity as the very reason for the existence of that theme or doctrine. God's love, care, and concern for humanity is reflected in the theme of creation, redemption, and atonement. There is no reason for the doctrines' existence if they are not connected to humanity. Themes and doctrines center on God but they teach us about God in relation to humanity, and not for the sake of merely gathering information about God. Flowery sermons about God's holiness or sovereignty may impress the educated and the illiterate alike, but they will do little to edify people who come to church to hear how this holy and sovereign God loves them and cares about the crises in their lives and communities. Preaching the themes of the Bible should develop congregations to intentionally care about and confront the social crises in their neighbor's community.

Preachers very seldom address social crises through their sermons on the themes of the Bible. Often these sermons promote theological arguments and doctrinal concerns, but they rarely bridge the gap between doctrines and matters pertaining to human life and existence. It is imperative that we keep the foundational tenets of our faith before the people of God. But their message is embraced, accepted, believed, and

---

12. Voth, 287.

practiced more faithfully when the preacher shows how these central tenets—kingdom of God, covenant, judgment, creation, atonement, and the sovereignty of God—connect to life issues, or more importantly, to the matters that threaten their lives. Preachers should not and cannot afford to leave theological themes and doctrines in the abstract. A sermon on creation that only deals with the majesty, power, and grandeur of God in creating the splendor of the galaxies and the beauty of earth falls short if it does not address the ugliness of war and the dearth in Third World countries (as not an intention of God's creation plan).

Preachers must ask these questions: What does creation have to do with dirty, lead-based water in Flint, Michigan? What does the theme of the fall have to do with crime, drugs, and poverty in a specific community? How can the members of my church see the sovereignty of God through the COVID-19 crisis? What have the covenants of Yahweh to do with immigration policies, for those who have loved ones in migration camps on the US border? Most believers struggle with the themes and doctrines of the Bible because they don't see how these fine theological arguments touch the things that matter to them.

For instance, preaching the theme of creation allows us to address the social concerns of environmental injustice (Gen 1:1, 31; Deut 11:13–17; Isa 33:7–10; Rom 8:18–25), human relationships (Gen 2:18–25; Matt 19:4–6), and racism (Gen 1:27; Ps 8:4–8; Acts 17:26–28). Frank Thielman reminds us that preaching on the substitutionary atonement should "remind Christians that they should not abuse their power, but should achieve greatness through service. . . . Because all people equally deserve God's wrath and are made right with God through Christ's death as a free gift, all should be treated equitably" (Rom 14:1–15:13).[13] Thielman makes the connection between the atoning sacrifice of Christ and our responsibility as Christians to address economic inequities, arguing there is biblical precedence "to find accounts of people in positions of wealth and power who surrendered part or all of their comfort to aid the weak because they took Jesus' death on the cross for the weak as their example."[14]

The biblical theme of the "day of the Lord" is not only an eschatological

---

[13.] Frank Thielman, "The Atonement," in *Central Themes in Biblical Theology: Mapping Unity in Diversity*, ed. Scott J. Hafemann and Paul House (Grand Rapids: Baker, 2007), 126.

[14.] Thielman, 126.

treatment of judgment at the end times. It has both a message of warning and celebration for the church in our present time. Paul House considers the day of the Lord as "both an exhortation to ethical living and a basis for hope."[15] Just as the day of the Lord presented divine judgment and punishment on rogue nations in the Prophets (Joel 1:15–18), the God who does not change is consistent in his warning to our political leaders who divide the nation, ignore the weak, and draft legislation that burdens the poor.

The Biblical Theme of Justice

From the opening pages of Scripture, we see justice as a thread that permeates and weaves through all that God does, and punctuates all that he is. God is just (Ps 89:14). In Scripture we see God's judgment on those who perpetuate injustice (Deut 27:19; Prov 6:16–19; Prov 11:1; Neh 4:4–5; Luke 11:42; Col 3:25). And we see his mercy extend to those who do justice (Prov 14:34; 21:15; Amos 5:24). God calls his people to "act justly, to love faithfulness" (Mic 6:8). This is because, as Bruce Birch notes, "Justice and righteousness describe persons and behaviors that seek wholeness and well-being for all, that seek equity in all social interrelationships, and that do not seek advantage at the expense of another's disadvantage."[16] This is what it means to "care about and confront the crises in our neighbor's community."

It is paramount to preach the theme of biblical justice, both for those who are denied justice and for those who have a secular idea of what justice is and should be. Social crisis preaching should not anchor its argument for justice in western Enlightenment rationalism. These forms of justice are rooted in individualism, justified by human reason alone, and anchored in relativism, void of any moral or divine absolutes. Social crisis preaching establishes justice as an attribute of God (Isa 28:6; Jer 9:24; Ezek 34:16). Preachers will challenge the congregation to exhibit justice (Deut 27:19; Ps 37:28). Preaching the theme of justice and calling for an application that requires congregations to

---

[15.] Paul House "The Day of the Lord," in *Central Themes in Biblical Theology: Mapping Unity in Diversity,* ed. Scott J. Hafemann and Paul House, (Grand Rapids: Baker, 2007), 183.

[16.] Bruce C. Birch in *Dictionary of Scripture and Ethics*, ed. Joel B. Green (Grand Rapids: Baker, 2011), 435.

seek justice for wrongs done to their neighbor is directly tied to them seeing their neighbor's worth.

Justice as a human quest seems elusive as the wind. Still, it is also an eternal, alluring Spirit, brooding over, drawing near, and calling forth those who yearn for him, sustaining them with the hope that their search for him will be found in God's promise. We live in an era where the cries of justice are more anguished and desperate than ever. As a result, the church faces two alarming extremes. On the one hand, these cries for justice fall on deaf ears and bounce off hearts, hard and cold with apathy, like irritants that disturb the everyday comforts of many.

On the other hand, and equally troubling, is that some cries are cloaked as calls for justice, but when unrobed, are exposed as actual shouts for revenge. They are void of mercy, blind to facts, and indifferent to repentance. Those who reflect this extreme can embody the very form of injustice they rail against. We long for the justice of God. These two extremes signal that preaching the theme of justice and bringing it to bear on contemporary social issues can be difficult but must not be avoided. Preachers will have to grapple with how to help congregations navigate between the biblical call for justice and the biblical mandate to forgive.

Justice and Forgiveness

On September 6, 2018, Botham Jean was shot and killed inside his apartment by Amber Guyger, an off-duty Dallas police officer. Jean, born in Saint Lucia, by all accounts, was a deeply committed Christian, an accountant, an upstanding, productive, and law-abiding citizen, known for his melodious voice as a singer in Harding University's choir and in his church choir at Dallas West Church of Christ. Guyger, a white female police officer, claimed to have mistaken Jean's apartment for her own. Figuring Jean to be an intruder, she fired shots that ended his life. Although this case garnered national attention, protest from across the nation, and cries for justice, what happened in the courtroom on October 2, 2019, the date after Guyger was found guilty of murder, not only shocked the world, but it shed light on the attitude of Christians in light of raging calls for justice when gross injustices have been inflicted.

During his victim-impact statement, Brandt Jean, the younger brother of Botham Jean, told the court that he forgives Guyger. He then looked to the judge and said, "I don't know if this is possible, but can I give her a hug, please?" After the judge granted permission, Brandt Jean then stepped down from the stand and embraced a tearful and seemingly sorrowful Guyger. Following the younger Jean's powerful display of grace, the presiding judge, Tammy Kemp, also stepped down from the bench to hug Guyger and gave her a Bible.[17] This was a powerful display of grace and redemption before a world experiencing a severe, painful racial divide.

Allison Jean, Botham Jean's mother, both praised her younger son's attitude of forgiveness, and rejoiced at Amber Guyger's conviction. Jean's mother also continued her cry for police reform and railed against police corruption. The question to explore when preaching about justice is, "Is Allison Jean's reaction and call for reform not as worthy of admiration as Brandt Jean's public forgiveness and embrace of Guyger?" Although the state asked for a twenty-eight-year prison sentence, Allison Jean expressed satisfaction with the ten-year sentence imposed by Kemp. She did not speak of forgiveness during her victim-impact statement, but of healing, and has filed a lawsuit against Guyger and the city of Dallas, and called for police training requirements. Allison Jean commented after the sentencing, "My son was much more valuable than 10 years. But there's nothing I can do about it."[18] Although many in the African American community respected Brandt Jean's decision to forgive his brother's killer, there was a deep fear that forgiveness, not justice, would become the expected remedy for racial healing. Forgiveness is an extension of grace. Grace should inspire and motivate obedience, not more sin (Rom 6:1–4). For a people with a track record of extending grace through offering forgiveness, the expected and hoped for response is to live in a world where one's skin color does not invite and incite violence. But when it does, we can demand and expect justice in the courts. African Americans are

---

17. Bill Chappell and Richard Gonzales, "Brant Jean's Act of Grace Toward Brother's Killer Sparks A Debate Over Forgiveness," *npr*, October 3, 2019, https://www.npr.org/2019/10/03/766866875/brandt-jeans-act-of-grace-toward-his-brother-s-killer-sparks-a-debate-over-forgi.

18. Darran Simons, "Botham Jean's mother says his life was more valuable than the 10 year sentence his killer received," CNN, October, 3, 2019, https://www.cnn.com/2019/10/03/us/botham-jean-mother-allison-jean/index.html.

rightfully concerned. As a community that has historically endured various forms of abuse and second-class citizenship, forgiveness as a biblical response to injustice has always been considered central—a necessary response, even when justice was not.

For most, the acts of mercy and forgiveness by Brandt Jean and Judge Kemp were heralded as an excellent model for how Christians should respond when wronged. For people who celebrate Jean's and Kemp's actions, this is the most admirable and, in some cases, the only Christian response to be celebrated. The words of Allison Jean, advocating for changes in police training and accountability of law enforcement officers and the police departments who employ them, are seldom viewed as Christian responses, and rarely celebrated as a part of biblical justice. Is preaching justice also preaching forgiveness? Does preaching forgiveness cancel or violate justice? When preaching about justice, is demanding punishment an applicable Christian response? What is the role of justice, forgiveness, atonement, and retribution? These are the penetrating questions that pastors must ask and pastorally guide congregations through. Some of these biblical themes are interrelated and should address social crises.

Anselm of Canterbury, the eleventh-century monk and theologian, poses a serious question for social crisis preachers and congregations. He asks, "What could be more just than for the good to receive good things and the wicked bad things?"[19] Anselm's belief in reciprocity and retributive justice seems antithetical to the teachings of forgiveness that fill the New Testament. But his question posed in an inductive sermon would propel the listener to wrestle with these questions biblically: What is the Christian's response towards the perpetrators of injustice? Must justice mean punishment for the perpetrator? Does the Christian's quest for justice include this punishment? What is the relationship between forgiveness and justice?

Concerning Anslem's views of reciprocity, Wolterstorff admits, "The reciprocity code, and the idea of punishment as retribution that goes along with it, have had such a tight grip on human thought and imagination that not even Jesus' rejection of the code and his injunction to

<hr>

[19.] Saint Anselm, *The Works of Saint Anselm*, Translated by Sidney Norton Deane, Digireads .com Publishing, chap. 10, Kindle Edition, Location 816 of 4395.

forgive rather than punish have been sufficient to loosen that grip."[20] Popular self-help books often say, forgiveness is not for the wrongdoer, but for those who have been wronged. I believe that is only partially true. Forgiveness is especially for those who have been wronged, but it is also for the wrongdoer. Being released and forgiven brings a sense of peace, joy, and an indescribable spirit of thanksgiving, both when it comes from God and when it comes from man. With the Spirit's help, we can shift our focus from punishment to rehabilitative justice for the perpetrator and restorative justice for the victim. Rehabilitative justice (not punishment) is not for the wrongdoer alone, but for the victims and those who may be potential victims of the wrongdoer's behavior, until the wrongdoer is rehabilitated.

When preaching justice, our answer is found at the cross of Christ. Sin required punishment. Jesus endured the punishment that we could not, but of which we were deserving. At the same time, forgiveness and grace were extended. Forgiveness does not mean that justice is negated. But justice, for a people who have been declared guilty since our conception, must not mean revenge, "because it is written, Vengeance belongs to me; I will repay, says the Lord (Rom 12:19b). Preaching the theme of justice teaches what biblical justice is and what it is not. Biblical justice is fairness and honesty (Exod 23:6; Lev 19:13); recognizes that wrongs must be made right (Exod 22:1; Lev 6:2–5; Luke 19); is mercy (Luke 18:1–8); calls us to consider the poor (Exod 22:22; Lev 19:15); and appeals to Christians to stand against systems and institutions that hurt, disenfranchise, and cause unfair treatment (Exod 3:7–12; Prov 11:1; Dan 3; Matt 21:12–13). We must preach biblical justice.

STORYTELLING AND NARRATIVE PREACHING

Ever since I could remember, my grandmother has been a master storyteller. She spent her final moments of life in a nursing home. Though strong in body, she was fragile in mind, as she was unable to even recall the faces of her children or grandchildren. But one thing she never forgot was her stories. Although dementia robbed her of the

---

[20]. Nicholas Wolterstorff, *Justice in Love* (Grand Rapids: Eerdmans, 2011), 193.

ability to connect with us, she could still hold us captivated with the vivid details of how molasses was made. She clearly described how hot it was to the touch and delicious to the taste it was for her as a child. Her stories were filled with color, details, and emotion. Her hands and facial expressions filled in the spaces where words fell short, thus in hearing the narrative, you felt as if you were there. I was amused by and in awe of her stories. Yet what I remember most is how I felt after hearing those stories. Both as a boy, and later as a man, whatever day we were blessed to hear one of them, for at least the rest of that day, and sometimes days later, my mind was fixed, consumed, and gripped, still rehearsing the details of the stories my bigmama told me.[21]

A good story sticks—it lingers, hovers, and remains in the soul and psyche, sometimes forever. Preaching narratively and incorporating storytelling in sermons can have that effect. Since preaching should lead to personal and communal transformation, storytelling allows the preacher to connect with the hearer on a more profound and lasting level. Stories have a way of sticking with people. When preaching is done narratively, the preacher can place the hearer in the story, making it profoundly transformative and deeply personal in its theology and principles.

We live in an era where visual learning is the dominant learning style, calling for visual presentations and image-induced teaching methods. Thus, it is no wonder that narrative preaching, also called the inductive style, is emerging again as a preaching style. Although narrative preaching received significant scholarly attention in the twentieth century, it has been a primary form of preaching in cultures and communities with strong oral histories, such as African American. Within the history of preaching, the narrative style emerged as a response to how congregations hear and grasp biblical truth, and as a reaction against dogmatic propositional preaching.

Commonly called the "New Homiletic," narrative preaching was championed by Eugene Lowry, Fred Craddock, David Buttrick, and others, each contributing various insights, methodologies, and principles to the discipline of narrative style preaching.[22] Narrative preaching

---

[21.] In the African American community, grandmothers are often referred to as "Bigmama." In the same sense, a grandfather is often referred to as "Bigdaddy."

[22.] See Fred B. Craddock, *As One Without Authority* (Nashville: Chalice, 2001); Eugene Lowry,

embodies storytelling, inviting listeners on an oral journey, where both preacher and listener arrive at the truth or big idea of the text at the end of the sermon. The narrative preacher uses "moves" within the sermon's structure to transport the listeners to the destination of truth in the text. So, rather than announcing the big idea and truths of the passage didactically amid the sermon, narrative preaching allows the listeners to discover the truths on their own. Effective narrative preaching includes conflict, tension, plot, and resolve.

Jesus taught eternal truths and their application through telling stories (Matt 13:3–9, 18–23; Mark 12:1–12; Luke 15:11–32). These stories provide social crisis preachers with an authoritative source to confront such topics as economic exploitation and greed in corporate entities (Luke 12:16–21), human discrimination (Luke 14:12–24), and individualism (Luke 11:5–8). Storytelling calls forth the three modes of persuasion of Greek oratory. In ancient classical Greek rhetoric, the ancient orator's rhetorical acumen was measured by his possession and utility of *ethos*, *logos*, and *pathos*. The rhetor's *ethos* was a testament to his moral fiber and perceived character, while *logos* had to do with logic and the speaker's ability to reason. Finally, *pathos* was measured by the orator's passion, emotional appeal, and ability to stir *pathos* in the hearer. Storytelling in Christian proclamation evokes emotions without manipulation.

In the movie *A Time to Kill*, Jake Brigance, an inexperienced lawyer, is sought out to defend Carl Lee Hailey, who is on trial for shooting the men who raped his young daughter. Brigance faces the improbable and almost impossible task of convincing an all-white jury in a segregated southern town to find Hailey's actions justifiable. In closing arguments, Brigance relies on a narrative that captivates the minds and hearts of not only those in the courtroom but the all-white jury—who was almost certain to find Carl Lee guilty of murder. Brigance asks the jury to close their eyes while he "tells them a story about a little girl, walking home from the grocery store one afternoon."[23]

With vivid detail, gut-wrenching particulars, and artistic rhetoric,

---

The Homiletical Plot: The Sermon as Narrative Art Form (Louisville: Westminster, 2001); David Buttrick, *Homiletic: Moves and Structures* (Philadelphia: Fortress, 1987).

[23.] *A Time to Kill*, directed by Joel Schumacher, (1996; United Kingdom: IMDb, 1996), Amazon Prime. Video.

Brigance teleports the jury into the very moment of the gruesome tragedy where the young girl was accosted and violated. He not only paints a horrendous picture of the tragedy, but he also connects the entire jury with Carl Lee, the loving, heartbroken, and desperate father. The verdict came back: not guilty. Perhaps, the attorney could have relied on physical evidence, witness statements, and a plethora of other logical defense strategies to defend his client. Instead, he turned the facts into a passionate, brilliantly told story.[24] Facts alone would not have been enough to persuade this jury. The attorney not only convinced the jury, but he led them to the truth. So narrative preaching should never be used to manipulate the hearers, but to transport them to the truth.

Three Functions of Narrative Preaching in the Social Crisis Sermon

There are several ways social crisis preaching moves from text to sermon by using a narrative preaching style. Narrative preaching enables preachers to creatively depict the background of the world behind the text to bring home the theology in the narrative. Background information opens the door for the preacher to deal with significant social issues related to those within the communities of the hearers. In his classic book on narrative preaching, *The Homiletical Plot*, Lowry lists ten "pointers in telling a story." Among the ten, the two that most adequately describe what I refer to as background information, are: "attend to every insignificant line" and "look between the lines."[25] Narrative preaching preaches the details of the text, the background information, and the setting in which the biblical writers exist.

Secondly, narrative preaching allows the listeners to identify with the characters in the text, for good or ill. In the African American church, enslaved Christians saw themselves in the slave experiences, the emancipation, and the wilderness wanderings of the Israelites. Herbert Robinson Marbury explains, "African Americans had few resources to resist the discursive force of written history and to

---

24. *A Time to Kill.*
25. Lowry, 107.

determine their own lives, but their religious imagination held trans-formative power."[26] With this cue and clue, social crisis preachers can clarify that God stands with oppressed communities, not with the empires that oppress them. In this way, the enslaved preacher was able to help the listeners see who they were in the text and whose attitude and actions (Pharoah or the Israelites) they more closely resembled. When preachers allow themselves to enter the narrative and permit their souls to soak in the world of the biblical author, surrendering their imaginations to the control of the Holy Spirit, their sermons will captivate the minds of the hearers long after they give the benediction. Hanna Meretoja suggests, "In weaving our experiences into stories, we make sense of them by linking them together into a meaningful account, by placing them within the context of our lives, the lives of others, and broader historical and cultural developments."[27] Narrative preaching is one effective social crisis preaching model. The truth of Scripture can be presented in narrative form, in ways the hearer can see and feel God's activity in their lives and communities.

Finally, narrative preachers can become artists and poets, using unforgettable words to transport the biblical truth from within the narrative of the Bible. Narrative preaching can serve the social crisis preacher well in the arduous journey from text to sermon.

Preaching the Background

Narrative preaching also allows the preacher to delve into the techni-cal details of the biblical culture, history, archaeology, topography, customs, dates, and literary details. All this information would be boring and lack relevance if given in any other context. A good sto-ryteller and narrative preacher gives attention to the background. The narrative preacher can make the technical topographical details, like the distance from Jerusalem to Jericho, a part of the story that pulls the hearer into the narrative to drive home a social crisis point. Reverend Dr. Martin Luther King, Jr., in his sermon "On Being

---

[26.] Herbert Robinson Marbury, *Pillars of Cloud and Fire: The Politics of Exodus in African American Biblical Interpretation* (New York: New York University, 2015), 5.
[27.] Meretoja, 100.

a Good Neighbor" speaks of the dangerous altruism of the Good Samaritan by telling the story of a trip to the Holy Land, in which he and his wife rented a car and traveled the Jericho Road. King states, "When Mrs. King and I visited the Holy Land, we rented a car and drove from Jerusalem to Jericho."[28] King describes the drive as a long, slow, descent down the mountainous terrain of Jericho. During the drive, it became obvious to King why the robbers chose this curvaceous road as the location to stage the heinous crime of robbery, given that Jerusalem is "some two thousand feet above and Jericho one thousand feet below sea level." The twist and turns of the Jericho Road put travelers at risk of surprise attacks from robbers lying in wait.

In most sermons on the Good Samaritan, the preacher's application generally focuses on replicating the Good Samaritan's attitude and action. But in King's sermon, by dealing with the background information, he connects the congregation with the attitudes and inactions of people who are not in the text, but nevertheless, very important in the mind of the biblical writer. King addresses the conditions of the Jericho Road and calls the listener to focus on why the road was so dangerous in the first place. In the sermon, King provides background details that would, in any other type of sermon, not have the impact as it does in this personal narrative. King's insertion of these details is not a rhetorical ploy, but instead, highlights the point that "it is also important to change the conditions which make robbery possible. Philanthropy is commendable, but it must not cause the philanthropist to overlook the circumstances of economic injustice which make philanthropy necessary."[29] In many American cities, crime and drugs are a cancer to the community. Yet we often lay the responsibility of eradicating crime on the economically deprived citizens that reside in those communities, without addressing the years of neglect in infrastructure, maintenance, and investments in lighting, parks, and recreation that are the responsibility of the municipalities that serve these communities.

[28.] Martin Luther King, Jr., *Strength to Love* (Boston: Beacon, 1963), 25–26.
[29.] King, 25.

Finding Identity in the Story

One of the most potent experiences in reading the Bible and listening to sermons is finding yourself as a sharer of the same sorrows, pain, joy, fears, and deliverance as those in the text. Bryan Chapell writes about the effectiveness of narrative preaching through shared experiences: "Through a story, listeners are introduced to an experience, vicariously live through the events or impressions described, and take away shared impressions of its implications so that meaning is formed and held in community."[30] There is a confidence that assures us that we are not alone in our grief and that God has traveled the same way of sorrow with others before us. In his wisdom, he ensured that his presence in the experiences of others was preserved in his Word for our edification. As much as we identify with David, Naomi, Joseph, Judas, and a host of others in the Bible, God, revealed in Jesus, is always the standard and the star of the narrative. James A. Sanders comments, "Biblical characters are not models for morality, but rather mirrors for identity."[31]

Identifying with biblical characters is not solely for individuals, but it is also a common practice of communities. Marbury contends, "In the early nineteenth century, many communities took the Bible's story of slavery and emancipation and made it black people's story of faith. Anguished black souls, both enslaved and free, angry and hopeful, adopted it as their own."[32] Social injustice rarely affects individuals alone; instead, it resonates, and its ripple effect sparks fear and hopelessness in those who identify with the victimized individual. The custom of life in America has been that disenfranchisement, oppression, and limited agency through voting rights and access to education affected groups. Whether those groups are minority racial groups identifying with the Israelites in the Old Testament, women identifying with the women of both Testaments, immigrants identifying with foreigners in the Old Testament, or disabled communities identifying with those deemed unclean, these Bible stories connect groups as sharers

---

[30.] Bryan Chapell, *Christ-Centered Preaching: Redeeming the Expository Sermon*, 2nd ed. (Grand Rapids: Baker, 2005), 164.

[31.] James A. Sanders, "Hermeneutics," in *The Interpreter's Dictionary of the Bible* (Nashville: Abingdon, 1976), 406.

[32.] Marbury, *Pillars of Cloud and Fire*, 13.

in God's redemptive narrative. Social crisis preachers must make these connections to instill hope and assurance in the lives of these groups of people. In seeing and feeling ourselves in these narratives, we are better able to see the hand of God in our deliverance. Meretoja finds, "The way in which we understand and narrate what was possible for the agents of past historical worlds affects how we understand what is and will be possible for the inhabitants of the current world."[33] When we can make these connections through narrative preaching, we have the opportunity to put on notice those who feel superior due to their physical prowess, tribal affiliation, or socioeconomic standing "that God is no respecter of persons" (Acts 10:34 KJV).

The Language of the People

Church history includes the bitter battles waged to produce the Bible in the language of the people. During the pre-Reformation period, advocates fought for ordinary people to have the Bible translated from the original languages into their native tongue. For this issue alone, some suffered greatly, even losing their lives. Preachers would benefit from remembering those sacrifices as they craft their sermons, by considering the words they choose to use. In his masterful book, *Social Crisis Preaching*, Smith Sr. warns, "Words are a part of the design of the sermon and sometimes they set the very tone for the reception of the sermon."[34] A story is only as effective as the storyteller's ability and willingness to use comprehensible and relatable language familiar to the recipients. Smith Sr. goes on to argue, "The use of high-sounding words with which the congregation is not familiar accomplishes no good."[35] Preaching cannot be so heady, scholastic, and void of the common vernacular that it fails to reach and touch the people in the pews. Contemporary language that makes the biblical story tangible, imminent, and easy to process makes social crisis preaching in narrative style effective.

For instance, Eugene H. Peterson, in *Tell It Slant*, writing about the

---

[33] Hanna Meretoja, *The Ethics of Storytelling: Narrative Hermeneutics, History, and the Possible* (Oxford: Oxford University, 2018), 95.

[34] Smith Sr., *Social Crisis Preaching*, 85 (see intro. n. 10).

[35] Smith Sr., 86.

lawyer in the parable of the Good Samaritan, advises that a more accurate rendering of "lawyer" in our day is not in the legal, courtroom
sense, but a religious professor or Bible scholar.[36] Drawing from another example of the "Good Samaritan" sermon, King uses phrases like
"Jericho Road Improvement Association," "life's roadside," "cataracts of
provincialism," and "life's Jericho Road." These are words with which
King's audience would have been familiar. Likewise, King uses exact
words to describe the Jericho Road like "sudden curves," "meandering,"
and "mountainous."[37] These words give a vivid picture of the narrative.

Most importantly, as indispensable pieces of the narrative sermon, these
familiar and precise words communicate the biblical truth and principles
embedded in the narrative. The details of the road become inseparable
from that truth and create a memorable, lasting impression on the hearer's
mind. People remember the story because of the words; therefore, the
truth, no matter how convicting or comforting, is inescapable.

THE WORLD IN FRONT OF THE TEXT

Before Elon Musk and Tesla, there was "KITT." As a young child in the
mid-1980s, one of my favorite television shows was "Knight Rider."[38]
The show, starring David Hasselhoff as Michael Knight, featured
Knight as a brilliantly trained crime-fighter along with his modern,
highly technological, artificially intelligent car "KITT," which stood
for Knight Industries Two Thousand. KITT had the ability to detect
danger, hold conversations, drive itself, and provide any computations
and information Knight may have needed. In 1984, imagining an
automobile capable of such feats was beyond most viewers' wildest
dreams. But for most engineers, automobile manufactures, and software
companies during the 80s, KITT's technological and almost-human
performance was well within reach. KITT projected possibilities, goals,
dreams, and ideals for automakers as the way things ought to be.

[36.] Eugene H. Peterson, *Tell It Slant: A Conversation on the Language of Jesus in His Stories and Prayers* (Grand Rapids: Eerdmans, 2008), 35.
[37.] Martin Luther King, Jr., "On Being a Good Neighbor," *A Gift of Love*, (UK: Penguin Classics, 2017), 21–31.
[38.] *Knight Rider*, creator Glen A. Larson, (1982–1986; UK: IMDb, 1985).

As a hermeneutical approach, the phrase "the world in front of the text" is like that. Biblical writers are projecting an ideal world for readers. By faith in the authority of the Word of God, such worlds, presented by the biblical author, are well within reach. As it relates to social crisis preaching, those who use this hermeneutical approach can address contemporary social crises by uncovering and revealing the world in front of the text to the congregation. This is a very effective means to confront social crises from the pulpit with biblical integrity. James Henry Harris states, "Getting in front of the text can help rescue preaching from the doldrums of past practices and ignite a flame of fire in the sermon that cannot be hidden or extinguished in the deep caves and crevices of the author's mind."[39] Getting in front of the text acknowledges that Scripture transcends geography, culture, and time and applies to worlds far removed from the biblical author, without losing the intent and meaning of its original impact. Social crisis preachers should preach the world in front of the text to identify and confront social crises in the present.

The phrase "in front of the text," claims Craig Bartholomew, is associated with "[Paul] Ricoeur and it refers to the world that opens up in front of the text as the reader engages with the text. It is to be distinguished from that which the text refers to, which Ricoeur describes as 'behind the text.'"[40] Although preaching must deal with "the world behind the text," preachers that stay stuck in the historical and cultural aspect of the biblical text will find it challenging to leverage the power of the text on the world of the hearers. The world in front of the text approach proves, as Abraham Kuruvilla aptly contends, "The text is given a future orientation, enabling valid application by readers at locations and times far removed from those of the event of inscription."[41] For social crisis preachers, this is vitally important, because the preacher is positioned to cast God's intended vision before a congregation ripe with social calamity and upheaval.

[39.] James Henry Harris, *Beyond the Tyranny of the Text: Preaching in Front of the Bible to Create a New World* (Nashville: Abingdon, 2019), 3.

[40.] Craig Bartholomew, "In Front of the Text: The Quest of Hermeneutics," in *The Bible in Pastoral Practice: Readings in the Place and Function of Scripture in the Church*, ed. P. Ballard and S. R. Holmes (Grand Rapids: Eerdmans, 2005), 136.

[41.] Abraham Kuruvilla, *Privilege the Text: A Theological Hermeneutic for Preaching* (Chicago: Moody, 2013), 27.

By proclaiming "the world in front of the text," preachers are not privileged to make up or create a utopia of their choosing, where they select facets of the world they desire to cater to so that they may comfort the concerns of the local church. Instead, preachers are bound to give strict attention to the author's intention, while providing precise significance and application for the contemporary audience. Consider the social crisis in the letter of James that is pictured in the biased attitudes of his readers toward the rich. The cultural standards they used to judge rewards and benefits are not a projection of God's intended vision for his creation. In other words, the significance of James's instruction to show no partiality to "a man wearing a gold ring and fine clothing" over "a poor man in shabby clothing" (Jas 2:2–4 ESV) is that we should not treat socioeconomically wealthy people with preferential treatment in any area of life, not just when they come "into your meeting wearing a gold ring and dressed in fine clothes." James projects a world in front of the text, in which his instructions will be applied beyond ecclesiastical settings. The application can be used to address the injustices that reside in the criminal justice system, where wealthy lawbreakers, though convicted, serve less jail time, solely because they can afford a good (expensive and well-connected) lawyer. Bryan Stevenson alarmingly admits, "In the American criminal justice system, wealth—not culpability—shapes outcomes. Many people charged with crimes lack the resources to investigate cases or obtain the help they need, leading to wrongful convictions and excessive sentences, even in capital cases."[42] James projects a world where the poor will not be judged and sentenced as guilty because they are poor.

The author's original intent is the anchor that holds the text's transcendent significance and application to the modern preacher's world. Since the Bible is the living Word of God, its message and the behaviors and ideals that God proclaims in it are intended for people of every era in time. In this way, the biblical authors, "as they were carried along by the Holy Spirit" (2 Pet 1:21), are not simply robotic transcribers or automated amanuenses, but those who intend for the inspired Word to be practiced and lived out in concrete, practical ways in the worlds of every future generation.

---

42. *Equal Justice Initiative*, "Criminal Justice Reform," 2022, https://eji.org/criminal-justice-reform/.

The social crisis preacher is responsible for investigating the social "world behind the text" to clearly see how the appropriate text develops congregations in the "world in front of the text," to intentionally care about and confront the social crises in their neighbor's community in the power of the Holy Spirit. James is projecting a world in which the rich and poor will be judged by the contents in their heart—by the weight of their generosity in acts of kindness—a world where "mercy triumphs over judgment" (Jas 2:13). Perhaps, this world that James creates with his words— "the world in front of the text" —is our first glimpse of King's beloved community.[43]

CONCLUSION

The cues and clues in Scripture enable preachers to help radically transform their congregations and local communities. The clues include a biblical author's shifting focus, exegetical insights, biblical themes, narrative preaching and storytelling, and the world in front of the text. The textual cues guide the preacher into a faithful interpretation and application, equipping congregations to better confront the social crisis where their neighbors live, work, and play. Our hermeneutics and exegetical studies have severe social implications. The quest for justice and human equity will be influenced by our commitment to work as servants of God, as we wait for the reign of Christ in the kingdom of God. Faithful exegesis should be paired with a redemptive paradigm for viewing the people of God. Faithful and effective preachers should interpret both Scripture and the people in the pew.

[43.] King's concept of the "beloved community" is rooted in the biblical concept of neighbor. King believed the beloved community is a global community, uninhibited by the boundaries of socioeconomic status and the myths of racial and ethnic superiority. For King, the quest for the beloved community is the responsibility of every person, thus the social, economic, and political struggles of any oppressed people invites the intervention and advocacy of the global community. In his speech concerning Ghana's independence, King's, "Birth of a Nation" speech, given March 6, 1957, a month after Ghana's independence captures the essence of the beloved community. King states, "The aftermath of violence is the creation of the beloved community. The aftermath of violence is redemption. The aftermath of violence is reconciliation." See, "Martin Luther King, Jr.'s Birth of a New Nation April 7, 1957," YouTube video, 35:03–35:13, https://www.youtube.com/watch?v=O1QaSFm6Hhk.

CHAPTER 2:

SACRED ANTHROPOLOGY

A Redemptive Paradigm for the People of God

What can pastors and preachers living in the twenty-first century learn from a Christian living in eighteenth century England to help the church bring redemption to one of America's most pressing social crises and alleviate human misery? John Howard was born September 2, 1726, in Hackney, London.[1] His life and work as a prison and social reformer remain a stellar and shining example of public theology and the inseparable relationship of spiritual rebirth and social impact. The mid-eighteenth-century jails and prisons throughout Europe were, according to Henry Fielding, "seminaries of vice and sewers of nastiness and disease."[2] Howard found passion and calling in changing these conditions. Inheriting wealth from his father, he traveled Europe and became high sheriff in Bedfordshire in 1773. In this role, Howard begin a lifetime commitment to change the living conditions of the town's most despised and marginalized, the prisoners in the Bedford jails.

In 1774, Howard persuaded the House of Commons to pass two acts that would grant release to persons who were acquitted of their crimes yet held in deplorable prison conditions because they could not pay the jailer to release them. The second act concerned the health and wellness of the prisoners. Howard proposed that justices

---

[1.] What is now Samford University, located in Homewood (Birmingham), Alabama, was founded as Howard College in Marion, Alabama, in 1841, and was named after John Howard.

[2.] Quoted from Michael Ignatieff, *A Just Measure of Pain: The Penitentiary in the Industrial Revolution* (London: Macmillan, 1978), 52.

should be responsible for the health of the prisoners.[3] But his care for prisoners and repulsion of inhumane prison and jail conditions were not limited to Bedford; he set out to reform prisons throughout Europe. Published in 1777, Howard's then groundbreaking work, *The State of the Prisons in England and Wales: With Preliminary Observations, and an Account of Some Foreign Prisons*, "notably its long fifth section, based on 553 prison visits carried out by Howard between late 1773 and the beginning of 1777, is credited with provoking a near instantaneous shift in opinion on penal questions among policymakers and the broader public," according to Neil Davie.[4] Howard's commitment to disrupt the normality of the acceptance of grim and detestable prison conditions was fueled by an *ethos* of Christian faith. His courage to challenge policies by proposing new concepts for how prisons were managed and how prisoners should be cared for was in keeping with a mandate from the gospel (Luke 4:18). What can we learn from Howard?

The United States of America has the largest prisoner population in the world.[5] Many of these prisoners live in deplorable conditions that can be described similarly to the prisons and jails in eighteenth century Europe, as "seminaries of vice and sewers of nastiness and disease."[6] In a report by Alabama Appleseed Center for Law and Justice, entitled "Deathtraps" the deplorable conditions of prisons in the state of Alabama are well documented:

[3] Neil Davie, "Feet of Marble or Feet of Clay?: John Howard and the Origins of Prison Reform in Britain, 1773–1790," *XVII-XVIII* [English], 76, 2019, mis en ligne le 31 décembre 2019, consulté le 12 février 2022, http://journals.openedition.org/1718/3446; DOI : http://doi.org/10.4000/1718.3446.

[4] Quoted from Davie, "Feet of Marble or Feet of Clay?" See John Howard, *The State of the Prisons in England and Wales: With Preliminary Observations and an Account of Some Foreign Prisons*, Cambridge Library Collection, British & Irish History, 17th & 18th Centuries (Cambridge: Cambridge University, 2013), doi:10.1017/CBO9781139891349.

[5] For world rankings of total prison populations by country see: *World Prison Brief*, "Highest to Lowest Prison Population Total," https://www.prisonstudies.org/highest-to-lowest/prison-population-total?field_region_taxonomy_tid=All. According to the Bureau of Justice Statistics report, produced by the U.S. Department of Justice in October 2020, the total US prison population was 1,430,800. See E. Ann Carson, "Prisoners in 2019," US Department of Justice, Bureau of Justice Statistics, Bulletin, October 2020, accessed February 12, 2020, https://bjs.ojp.gov/content/pub/pdf/p19.pdf. See also, *Equal Justice Initiative*, "Criminal Justice Reform," https://eji.org/criminal-justice-reform/.

[6] Quoted from Ignatieff, *A Just Measure of Pain*, 52.

The Alabama prison system has been in crisis for nearly fifty years. In 2019, the United States Department of Justice (DOJ) released a 56–page report that detailed intense physical and sexual abuse, corruption, and rampant drug use, stating that the ADOC "has violated and is continuing to violate the Eighth Amendment rights of prisoners housed in men's prisons by failing to protect them from prisoner-on-prisoner violence, prisoner on-prisoner sexual abuse, and by failing to provide safe conditions . . . ."[7]

In addition to the unconscionable conditions in the Alabama prisons, many inmates are serving life sentences for crimes in which there was no physical injury. Some of these inmates are now faithful followers of Christ, have lived in prison honor dorms, and have been without any prison offenses, but are now old and destined to die in prison.

Pastors, preachers, and Christians in the pews of America's churches can model the *ethos* of John Howard by advocating for the image-bearers in America's prisons. In addition, the social crisis of injustice in America's prisons has racial ramifications. In the United States, according to the US Department of Justice, "The imprisonment rate of black adults (1,446 per 100,000 black adult US residents) at year end 2019 was more than five times that of white adults (263 per 100,000 white adult US residents)."[8] The same report provides another heart-wrenching statistic: "Black males ages 18 to 19 were 12 times as likely to be imprisoned as white males of the same ages, the highest black-to-white racial disparity of any age group in 2019."[9] As it relates to the inhumane and violent prisons in Alabama, Black inmates are more likely to be victims of violence. Alabama Appleseed Center for Law and Justice reports, "There were 48 homicides in Alabama's prisons between June 2014 and September 2020. Thirty-seven of the individuals who died by

---

[7.] Alabama Appleseed Center for Law and Justice, "Deathtraps: An Examination of the Routine and Violent Deaths of People in the Custody of the State of Alabama, 2014–2020," accessed February 12, 2022, https://www.alabamaappleseed.org/wp-content/uploads/2020/11/Death-Traps -Report-2020–FINAL.pdf, See also, Helling 509 U.S. qtd. in the United States Department of Justice Investigation into the Conditions of Alabama's Prisons for Men. 2019.

[8.] Carson, "Prisoners in 2019."

[9.] Carson, "Prisoners in 2019," p. 16.

homicide were Black, and eleven were white. Black men in Alabama prisons are 3.3 times more likely to be killed than their white
counterparts."[10] The life and work of the eighteenth-century prison
reformer John Howard speaks to the work of the twenty-first century sacred anthropologist. Howard's work and the Christ-honoring
work of the sacred anthropologist offer a paradigm of redemption
that addresses a myriad of social crises, including social injustice in
prisons and the problems associated with racism.

Race and the haunting complexities of racism continue to beset
the nation in which we live. There are a plethora of examples of racial tension in our nation and church. The current debate on critical
race theory reveals that the majority of African Americans feel firmly
convinced that there is value in it, while the majority of white Americans have rallied around their legislative and executive branches in
Southern states to issue bans on it.[11] In 2020, the debate over the
removal of Confederate statues and monuments saw Americans taking
sides, primarily along racial lines. The majority of African Americans
were in favor of the removal of the monuments from public spaces,
while the majority of white Americans were in favor of allowing the
monuments to stay in place. Racial tension abounds in the church
and the country due to the recent shootings of African Americans
by police officers, and other seemingly racially motivated murders
where African Americans have been the victims. In 2020, George
Floyd, Breonna Taylor, Kurt Reinhold, and Andre Hill, all Black, all
unarmed, were murdered by police, sparking outrage among Black
communities nationwide. That same year, racial tensions rose when
Ahmaud Arbery was killed after being confronted by three white men

10. Alabama Appleseed Center for Law and Justice, "Deathtraps."

11. Critical race theory (CRT) is an interdisciplinary intellectual discipline that examines the
intersection of race and law in the United States. CRT is over forty years old and was developed
by legal scholars. The pioneers are Derrick Bell, Kimberlé Crenshaw, and Richard Delgado, among
others. See Gary Peller, Kimberlé Crenshaw, Neil Gotanda, and Kendall Thomas, *Critical Race
Theory: The Key Writings That Formed the Movement* (New York: New Press, 1995) and Richard
Delgado and Jean Stefancic, *Critical Race Theory: The Cutting Edge, 3rd ed.*, (Philadelphia: Temple
University, 2013). At this writing, all fourteen members of the Mississippi State Senate walked
out before the final vote on a bill to ban teaching critical race theory in schools and universities.
The vote passed 32–2. If the Mississippi bill is enacted into law, the state will join nine other states
banning the teaching of critical race theory. See, Rashawn Ray and Alexandra Gibbons, "Why
Are States Banning Critical Race Theory?" *Brookings*, November 2021, accessed January 3, 2021,
https://www.brookings.edu/blog/fixgov/2021/07/02/why-are-states-banning-critical-race-theory/.

claiming that Arbery was the culprit in a string of burglaries in the Satilla Shores neighborhood, near Brunswick, Georgia. Perhaps, the most glaring example of racial tension centered around the presidency of Donald Trump.

In the 2020 elections, 87 percent of African Americans voted for Joseph Biden, while only 12 percent voted for Donald Trump. African Americans have been critical of Trump's racial rhetoric as well as his positions on Confederate monuments, endorsement of militant groups, and reluctance to propose and champion criminal justice reform. Social crisis preaching addresses the problems of race in our world, but takes a redemptive approach through the sacred anthropologist, in how Christians are to view and treat other image-bearers. It is impossible to write a book on social crisis preaching without addressing one of the major symptoms of social crisis in society and the church.[12] Edmondson and Brennan raise a sobering statement, followed by an even more penetrating question, "The racial hierarchy in the United States could not have been built and sustained without the active and passive support of millions of Christians. Why do you think so many Christians have supported racial injustice throughout US history?"[13] This question begs to be asked by the social crisis preacher as sacred anthropologist.

This chapter will provide a redemptive view of race through the practices of the sacred anthropologist, by articulating a pastoral theology for social crisis preaching. Effective preaching requires preachers to exegete the people in the pews as faithfully as the preaching text. Exegeting people entails understanding the people who hear our sermons. The

---

[12.] While I do not intend to be exhaustive, I will focus on a specific aspect of race, namely the way in which it has negatively impacted the church. See Mary Beth Swetnam Mathews, *Doctrine and Race* (Tuscaloosa: University of Alabama, 2017); Carolyn Renée Dupont, *Mississippi Praying: Southern White Evangelicals and the Civil Rights Movement, 1945–1975* (New York: NYU, 2013); Donald Mathews, *At the Altar of Lynching: Burning Sam Hose in the American South* (Cambridge: Cambridge University, 2018); Michael O. Emerson and Christian Smith, *Divided By Faith: Evangelical Religion and the Problem of Race in America* (New York: Oxford University, 2001); Richard A. Bailey, *Race and Redemption in Puritan New England* (New York: Oxford University, 2014); Rebecca Anne Goetz, *The Baptism of Early Virginia: How Christianity Created Race* (Baltimore: Johns Hopkins University, 2016); Jemar Tisby, *The Color of Compromise: The Truth about the American Church's Complicity in Racism* (Grand Rapids: Zondervan, 2020); and J. Russell Hawkins, *The Bible Told Them So: How Southern Evangelicals Fought to Preserve White Supremacy* (New York: Oxford University, 2021).

[13.] Edmondson and Brennan, *Faithful Anti-Racism*, 85 (see intro, n. 14).

pastor, acting as sacred anthropologist, can be the agent of change the church longs for in these painful hours when racial tensions are dividing God's church once again.

First, racism is a painful thorn in America's side, the Achilles' heel in the march for justice and equality. It would be irresponsible to address social crises without equipping the reader with the necessary tools to effectively lead the church out of the dark and long night of racial division and injustice into the light of a new day as "the light of the world" (Matt 5:14). To write about racism is to confront it. We cannot hide, nor must we make the grave past mistake of ignoring it.

Second, I am firmly convinced that the church must be the leader in providing the diagnosis and prescription for the race problem in our world. We have the tools. We have the Word of God and the Holy Spirit (Eph 6:17). While the church played a major part in leading the country out of slavery and the Jim Crow era, we must answer the call again. The social crisis preacher acting as sacred anthropologist is a way forward to a brighter and more just tomorrow.

From 2014–2020, several unarmed African Americans died at the hands of police officers; among the most notable were Eric Garner, Philando Castile, Nathaniel Pickett II, Ronell Foster, and Tony M. Green.[14] Undoubtedly, such cases result in much controversy and elicit a variety of responses. Having police in my congregation, I learned that their family members and loved ones could hold fundamentally different opinions and perspectives around such events. One household could include a mother who identifies with the grief experienced by a parent of a shooting victim. In the same home is a socially progressive university student who engages from the standpoint of an activist on

---

[14.] On July 17, 2014, Eric Garner was killed by Daniel Pantaleo, an NYPD officer who used a chokehold to subdue Garner while arresting him on suspicion of selling single cigarettes. Since Garner was not in possession of ten thousand cigarettes or four hundred pounds of tobacco, under NY State Tax Law § 1814, his crime would have been a misdemeanor. Philando Castile was shot by Jeronimo Yanez, a Minneapolis-area police officer, on July 6, 2016, during a traffic stop. Yanez pulled over the car, driven by Castile's girlfriend Diamond Reynolds, for a broken taillight. Nathaniel Picket II was shot by a San Bernardino County, California, sheriff's deputy in 2015; Picket suffered from mental illness, was unarmed, and less than one hundred feet from his front door at the time of the shooting. Ronell Foster was shot and killed by the police in Vallejo, California, in 2018 after being stopped for riding his bicycle without a light. Tony M. Green, Jr. was shot and killed by a Kingsland police officer on June 20, 2018, following a traffic stop.

her college campus. To top it off, the father is a twenty-year career police captain who intimately knows the complexities and dangers of protecting and serving one's community. How is the preacher to address such an event from the pulpit?

When this family is in the pews, the social crisis preacher must be responsible and wise, knowing that deep familial fractures could occur when addressing such events. The proclamation of biblical truth can be damaging if preaching is done ignorantly, void of sensitivity, and laced with legalistic undergirding. At the same time, the preacher must not compromise the truth, skirt around the issue, or be indecisive about the prophetic witness Christians are called to bear on these matters that affect the existence and everyday lives of the people in our pews. I learned to be very decisive, confront the subject with compassion and grace, and lead my congregation in developing a heart for our neighbors. By cultivating our affections to respect others, we can serve as a cultural resource for those who may differ from us, even if they live under the same roof.

Buttrick, in his classic text *Homiletic*, contends, "True Christian preaching is not only a hermeneutic of texts, but a hermeneutic of human situations."[15] Effective preachers know and understand their hearers. One must exegete both the text at hand and the pew before them. Exegeting the pews is central to preaching, but most crucial for social crisis preaching. We cannot begin to get into the nuts and bolts of social crisis preaching without laying a sound foundation in this area. The social crisis preacher is, in effect, a scared anthropologist. My definition of a **sacred anthropologist** is one who:

1. **recognizes** their presuppositions (about the biblical text and people),
2. while showing **respect** to their neighbor, by
3. **resisting** myths about their neighbor, and
4. by serving as a **resource** of truth for their church and community,
5. while challenging the congregation to **respond** by intentionally caring for and confronting the crises in their neighbor's community.

[15.] David Buttrick, *Homiletic*, 405 (see chap. 1, n. 22).

We might refer to these actions as the five Rs of the sacred anthropologist: recognize our presuppositions; respect our neighbor; resist
the myths; be a resource for others; and call for an intentional response
from the congregation. I will further develop each part in this chapter.

This pastoral theology will inform pastors and preachers of their
functionality as sacred anthropologists in the social crisis preaching
process. I will construct this pastoral theology by building on the
image of an anthropologist and developing on a specific field of anthropology: cultural anthropology. By using insights from the cultural
anthropologist while maintaining a Christological anthropology, the
social crisis preacher emerges as a "sacred anthropologist." Christological anthropology addresses what it means to be human in light of the
Scriptures' testimony that man is made in the image of God. More
specifically, Christological (Christ) *anthropos* (human) speaks to God's
intent for his creation living and being in Christ (Acts 17:28; 2 Cor
5:17). What makes the preacher's anthropological insights "sacred" is
the Word of God.

Sacred anthropologists differ from cultural anthropologists by satu-
rating the insights of cultural anthropology in the sacred truth of the
Bible. An anthropologist studies humans and uses that to solve human
problems. A sacred anthropologist, with God's help, communicates
God's Word and truth to fallen people—helping people understand
who God says they are, and how to live and exist as a result of it. A
sacred anthropologist is a tool in the hand of God to lead God's people
in this world, the only one who can lead people to lasting solutions to
the world's problems (spiritual and social). A sacred anthropologist is
an understudy of the Creator of humanity (*anthropos*). Only God can
grant us insight on the human condition. He reveals to us in Christ
what it means to be truly human (Rom 5).

The American Anthropological Association defines their task as "dedicated to advancing human understanding and applying this understanding to the world's most pressing problems."[16] For the social crisis
preacher, this statement is true yet incomplete. Human understanding
is indeed vital for solving the world's most pressing problems. But

---

16. For more information about AAA, see: https://www.americananthro.org/ConnectWithAAA
/Content.aspx?ItemNumber=1665&navItemNumber=586.

human understanding alone is insufficient for world-sized problem-solving. Restricting resolution of the world's problems to mere "human understanding and knowledge," places the sole responsibility on frail and fallen humanity, whose efforts will not last. This approach borders on humanism, which places emphasis and dependence on the human rather than the divine. Humanists place value, importance, and virtue in human beings and seek to solve problems through rational means and a confident hope in human goodness. History testifies that the mere understanding and knowledge of cultures and peoples, without the superintending power of the Word and Spirit of God, have often led to the exploitation, denigration, and destruction of people and civilizations. History has shown that humanity, left to its own devices and resources, can commit atrocious acts (enslavement, civil wars, the Holocaust, to name a few). The historical record also reflects that humanity has been the agent of goodness in the world. But humans, whether one acknowledges it or not, are limited beings. Left to their own devices, they place the world's future in frail and faulty hands.

To solve the world's most pressing problems, we must accept the claims of God's Word concerning humanity as true. This serves as the epistemological foundation of our understanding of humanity. The preacher, as sacred anthropologist, works to apply this scripturally induced understanding by excavating buried biblical truth (exegesis) and mining and examining historical and cultural data (understanding their congregation's world). This, in turn, will lead to understanding God's people, granting them a greater awareness of God's unfolding story of the redemption in Christ.

As an anthropologist probes the earth for clues of ancient civilizations, the preacher, as a sacred anthropologist, must dig and mine for cultural truths amid mountains of misconceptions and layers of lies. Developing the tools to pick apart and break up the fallow, dry, cold ground of compressed half-truths can be daunting. The broken tools of flawed exegetical practices and racist anthropology, introduced by previous generations of preachers and passed down to us, have proven to be dull, slow, and incapable of removing the underbrush of cultural ignorance and bias.[17] Thus, it is responsible for choking out the fresh

---

[17.] The Southern Baptist Theological Seminary published the "Report on Slavery and Racism

growth of justice, harmony, and reconciliation in our churches and communities. But in developing these tools, the sacred anthropologist, as a social crisis preacher, is able to better understand God's people and is more capable of communicating God's word to a variety of people.

THE SACRED ANTHROPOLOGIST AS SOCIAL CRISIS PREACHER

The preacher must be a sacred anthropologist. As stated above, there are five steps to becoming a sacred anthropologist in the pulpit: one who (1) recognizes their own presuppositions, (2) respects their neighbor, (3) resists the myths associated with their neighbor, (4) who is a resource of truth for their church and community, (5) while challenging their congregation to respond to crises, by intentionally caring about and confronting the crises in their neighbor's community. Let us examine each aspect in detail.

STEP 1: RECOGNIZING PRESUPPOSITIONS: CHECKING OURSELVES

Everyone has presuppositions when approaching the biblical text. Craig Blomberg clearly explains, "Anyone who claims to have no presuppositions and who studies the Bible objectively and inductively is either deceived or naïve."[18] There is no possibility in which an interpreter reads the biblical text presuppositionless. The preacher must recognize—not ignore —their presuppositions. Nor should one pretend that, as hard as one tries, they do not exist. Acknowledging that our denominations, traditions, experiences, cultures, and theological education shape how we interpret Scripture is unquestionably essential. The sermons and

---

in the History of the Southern Baptist Theological Seminary" in late 2017. This report, conducted by six scholars, testified to the fact that all the seminary's founding faculty held slaves and defended slaveholding. The seminary's faculty also opposed racial equality. Southern Baptist Theological Seminary President Albert Mohler writes in the introduction of the report, "Many of their successors on this faculty, throughout the period of Reconstruction and well into the twentieth century, advocated segregation, the inferiority of African Americans, and openly embraced the ideology of the Lost Cause of southern slavery." See https://sbts-wordpress-uploads.s3.amazonaws.com/sbts/uploads/2018/12/Racism-and-the-Legacy-of-Slavery-Report-v4.pdf, 2.

[18.] William W. Klein, Craig L. Blomberg, and Robert L. Hubbard, Jr., *Introduction to Biblical Interpretation, Revised and Updated* (Nashville: Thomas Nelson, 2004), 143.

Bible lessons I heard as a child always had personal salvation as well as personal responsibility as points of application. My community of faith found in our interpretation of Scripture, Jesus as redeemer, but also one who served as an example of how we should advocate for the poor and minorities. For example, in African American church culture, a commitment to theological truth includes a commitment to justice. "Black churches," writes Peter Paris, "viewed justice, improving the quality of the race's life, as grounded in the truth, that is the will of the Redeemer."[19] The African Methodist Episcopal denomination was birthed from Richard Allen's and Absalom Jones's fervent fidelity to Scripture amid the constant ostracism and rejection of the Methodist Episcopal Church. These historical experiences of rejection led to this denomination's conviction that the Bible advocates for spiritual and social liberation for all people.

Presuppositions do not only exist when one interprets Scripture. As we all know, it is not just Christians who hold presuppositions. We humans have presuppositions when it comes to engaging with people who are "not like us." Christians, albeit preachers, are not exempt from this reality. Do we hold stereotypical presuppositions about the disabled, women, poor, rich, or those from other faith traditions or denominations? When it comes to people, how do we distinguish between presuppositions and stereotypes? Are they the same? Whether our presuppositions concern the biblical text or the people in the pews, it is imperative in social crisis preaching to recognize and distinguish between healthy and unhealthy ones. Healthy presuppositions contribute positively to the body of Christ. Unhealthy ones are false, stereotypical, rooted in fear and ignorance, often baseless, and from flawed sources. Healthy presuppositions advocate for the inherent equality in all races and ethnicities. Unhealthy ones maintain that some races are superior physically, intellectually, and morally, and attempt to find biblical justification for their convictions. For the sacred anthropologist, whether interpreting the text or the pews, recognizing our own presuppositions as a preacher can best be accomplished by (1) appreciating the positive presuppositions of other biblical faithful communities and (2) accepting our own positive presuppositions.

[19.] Peter J. Paris, *The Social Teaching of the Black Churches* (Philadelphia: Fortress, 1985), 75.

Appreciating Other Interpretive Communities

The first element of recognizing our presuppositions is to appreciate other faithful interpretive communities. Although there are foundational and imperative principles and presuppositions that are non-negotiable within Christian biblical interpretation, such as the authority and infallibility of Scripture, there is no denomination or faith tradition that has a monopoly on biblical interpretation. Matthew Kim states, "Preaching can be error-prone when we read the text only from our limited cultural point of reference."[20] Each person, local church, and denomination brings presuppositions to reading and interpreting Scripture, influenced by their social locations, experiences, and traditions, both for good and evil. In the act of interpreting Scripture, readers are influenced, for good and ill, by their social locations, experiences, and traditions. All presuppositions are not inherently evil. Some contribute positively to how we live out our faith, by showing Christian love to one another. We can appreciate and learn much from the Christian communities whose lives and journeys have been marked by faithful adherence to the Bible as the Word of God. The sacred anthropologist must be wise to appreciate the interpretation of Scripture from other faithful communities in the body of Christ. In this book about social crisis preaching, I must highlight that an appreciation for the interpretive practices of people whose lives have been marked and marred by social crises is needed.

Learning from the African American Preacher and Congregation

Suppose the litmus test for sound and orthodox biblical interpretation in our preaching is found living in the face of social crises. In that case, the African American church community stands as an exemplar faith community. Cleophus LaRue explains, "The distinctive power of black preaching is to be found, first and foremost, in that which blacks believe Scripture reveals about the sovereign God's involvement in the everyday affairs and circumstances of their marginalized

---

[20.] Matthew D. Kim, *Preaching with Cultural Intelligence: Understanding the People Who Hear Our Sermons* (Grand Rapids: Baker, 2017), 15.

existence."[21] The Black preaching tradition has used a hermeneutic that informs them on how the finer points of theology and doctrinal discourse affect people who have been the object of excruciating harm, neglect, and injustice in their lives. This hermeneutic is founded in their positive presupposition that the Bible consistently casts God as being on the side of the weak, vulnerable, and exploited. By learning from this strand of the African American church tradition, one takes away that orthodoxy and orthopraxy go hand in hand. Thus, one must argue against any proclamation that extols the components of fine theology yet communicates a thoroughly anemic anthropology, void of addressing how sin affects people's lives. Any hermeneutical method that utterly divorces what God has said from how God calls his people to live is no Christian hermeneutic at all.

During the eighteenth and nineteenth centuries, theologians trained at the finest universities held presuppositions that led to a concocted hermeneutic that maintained the inferiority of Black enslaved persons. They insisted, both from exegesis and exercise, that slavery was divinely ordained and biblically sound. Howard Thurman accurately assesses how skewed some dominant interpretations of the Bible can become. He says

> for it reveals to what extent a religion that was born of a people acquainted with persecution and suffering has become the cornerstone of a civilization and of nations whose very position in modern life has too often been secured by a ruthless use of power applied to weak and defenseless people.[22]

Nevertheless, illiterate enslaved persons, who were governed by and moved by the Spirit, pushed back on the interpretive errors of the erudite white scholars. Esau McCaulley contends that the enslaved interpreters "rejected this categorization of Blacks as less than human, and thereby claimed the same exemption from slavery that applied to the rest of God's creation."[23] The abolitionist era produced a cavalry of

---

[21.] Cleophus J. LaRue, *The Heart of Black Preaching* (Louisville: Westminster, 2000), 2.

[22.] Howard Thurman, *Jesus and the Disinherited* (Boston: Beacon, 1976), 11.

[23.] Esau McCaulley, *Reading While Black: African American Biblical Interpretation as an Exercise in Hope* (Downers Grove, IL: IVP Academic, 2020), 19.

the formerly enslaved who wrote slave narratives that remain some of the most poignant and descriptive pieces of American literature. These firsthand accounts describe the dehumanizing characterizations thrust upon them and the faith-filled resolve required to resist these false narratives. One of the most important voices from the mid-nineteenth century came in the form of the only extant narrative by a Black indentured servant. Harriet Wilson's narrative, *Our Nig*, captures the abuse she endured, and articulates how Christian proclamation and witness sought to exclude Blacks at every turn. Wilson writes

> Frado, under the instructions of Aunt Abby and the minister, became a believer in a future existence—one of happiness or misery. Her doubt was, is there a heaven for the black? She knew there was one for James, and Aunt Abby, and all good white people; but was there any for blacks? She had listened attentively to all the minster said, and all Aunt Abby had told her; but then it was all for white people.[24]

An equally powerful slave narrative is that of Olaudah Equiano, a prince who was kidnapped from present-day Nigeria, who later became a faithful Christian and British abolitionist. His slave narrative brings a ringing indictment on the dehumanization of slavery, as he communicates the common thoughts that ran through the minds of thousands of slaves, that death was often preferable than life in slavery. He states

> At the sight of this land of bondage, a fresh horror ran through all my frame, and chilled me to the heart. My former slavery now rose in dreadful review to my mind, and displayed nothing but misery, stripes, and chains; and in the first paroxysm of my grief, I called upon God's thunder, and his avenging power, to direct the stroke of death to me, rather than permit me to become a slave, and to be sold from lord to lord.[25]

[24.] Harriet E. Wilson, *Our Nig: Or, Sketches from the Life of a Free Black,* 150th Anniversary Edition, (New York: Penguin, 2009), 47. The original manuscript was published in 1859 by Geo. C. Rand and Avery in Boston.

[25.] Olaudah Equiano, *The Life of Olaudah Equiano, or Gustavus Vassa, the African* (Mineola, NY: Dover, 1999), 69.

Equiano also testifies to the healing power of the Word of God and its affirming presence in light of the abuses endured by Christian slave masters. He testifies about how he learned of God's love through reading the Bible: "The Bible was my only companion and comfort; I prized it much, with many thanks to God that I could read it for myself, and was not left to be tossed about or led by man's devices and notions."[26] The Bible affirmed his humanity, when his slave master did not.

The most notable of the slave narratives is *Narrative of the Life of Frederick Douglass.* Douglass, perhaps the most powerful and influential African American leader of the nineteenth century, shines a bright light on the hypocrisy of slaveholding Christianity. Douglass affirms and commends the virtues of the Christian faith but despises the hypocrisy of the professed Christians who abused him. With sheer honestly and sincerity he confesses

> For, between the Christianity of this land, and the Christianity of Christ, I recognize the widest possible difference—so wide that to receive the one as good, pure, and holy, is of necessity to reject the other as bad, corrupt, and wicked. To be the friend of one is of necessity to be the enemy of the other. I love the pure, peaceable, and impartial Christianity of Christ; I therefore hate the corrupt, slaveholding, women-whipping, cradle-plundering, partial and hypocritical Christianity of this land. Indeed, I can see no reason, but the most deceitful one, for calling the religion of this land Christianity.[27]

Douglass's faith compelled him to labor with white and Black Christian abolitionists, speaking and writing against slavery, the rights of women, and the formerly enslaved. Wilson, Equiano, and Douglass rejected narratives that defined them as less than image-bearers. With their own narratives, they boasted about freedom in Jesus Christ and from the tyranny of the systemic evil, contrary to the redemptive purposes of God for his people. The faith of these three gospel-carrying human beings resounds in the theme of social crisis preaching: "to compassionately care

---

[26.] Equiano, 145.
[27.] Frederick Douglass, *Narrative of the Life of Frederick Douglass, an American Slave, Written by Himself,* ed. David Blight (Boston: Bedford, 1993), 105.

for and radically confront social crises in the communities where their neighbors live, work, worship, and play." Christians of every ethnicity and race can embrace the same fervor to fight against forms of injustice that threaten the life, freedom, and humanity of God's people.

When one surveys the largest white Christian denomination and the largest Black Christian denomination, the doctrinal tenets and the structures of belief are strikingly similar.[28] When one studies the tradition of preaching within these two Baptist denominations, both view the Bible as the Word of God, authoritative and powerful. But the difference lies in the experiences and social location of those within each community, thus affecting their interpretation and application of Scripture. In the same Scriptures, Black preachers saw the spiritual and social liberation of those facing communal social crises. The Black preacher's understanding of how God acts on behalf of suffering communities is derived from their singularly distinct social location, as a part of an oppressed community that has encountered God in those realities.

African American preachers have traditionally held a high view of Scripture. As Henry H. Mitchell attests, "Black preaching has been centered in the Bible throughout its history. Black congregations do not ask what a preacher's personal opinion is. They want to know what God has said through the preacher's encounter with the Word."[29] So, historically, the African American preacher's primary presupposition is the authority of the Bible as the Word of God.

Further tethered to this presupposition is the notion that the Bible has a particular message to the poor, oppressed, and socially vulnerable. Thus, the preacher is bound to proclaim that message, not above or distinct from salvation, but alongside it. The Gospel is the good news to the poor and the oppressed, thus the social ramifications are inherent in the spiritual content of the Gospel's message for salvation. The

---

[28.] The Southern Baptist Convention is the largest protestant denomination in the world, with 47,592 churches and 14,089,947 members; 39,755 of their church/congregations are Anglo. The SBC, though not a credal denomination, articulates their fundamental theological beliefs in the Baptist Faith and Message. See: https://bfm.sbc.net/bfm2000/. The National Baptist Convention, USA, Inc. is the largest African American denomination, boasting 21,145 churches and 8,415,100 members. See the "What We Believe" tab, which includes their Articles of Faith and their position statements at https://www.nationalbaptist.com/about-nbc/what-we-believe.

[29.] Henry H. Mitchell, *Black Preaching: The Recovery of a Powerful Art* (Nashville: Abingdon, 1990), 6.

African American Christian community sees the social application of the gospel message as a given. The Gospel is the good news to the poor and the oppressed, thus the social ramifications are inherent in the spiritual content of the Gospel's message for salvation. This is a presupposition worthy of appreciation. What would have happened if the slave master who believed on biblical grounds that enslaved persons were inferior suddenly embodied humility, listened to, and accepted the message of the enslaved preacher? What would this Christian testimony say to the world amid the atrocities and inhumane conditions of American slavery?

Accepting Our Positive Presuppositions

Secondly, we need not assume that all our presuppositions should be avoided, or that all our presuppositions are unhealthy and harmful. We also have positive presuppositions. To draw again from McCaulley, "If we all read the biblical text assuming that God is able to speak a coherent word to us through it, then we can discuss the meanings our varied cultures have gleaned from the Scriptures."[30] When we are honest, sincere, and commit to the sweat-work of exegetical labors with the Holy Spirit as our guide, our presuppositions can be corrected, because as we read the text, the text also interprets us, and we are changed by it. Anthony Thiselton comments, "Texts can actively shape and transform the perceptions, understanding, and actions of readers and of reading communities."[31]

We all have experiences that are common to humanity, but we also have unique experiences. God created humanity in his image: "From one man he has made every nationality to live over the whole earth" (Acts 17:26a). Yet we hold our distinctions and diversity as expressions of a powerful and omniscient Creator, who sojourns with all people, revealing himself through his Son to all. This reality is culminated in the grand eschatological vision expressed by John: "I looked, and there was a vast multitude from every nation, tribe, people, and language, which no one could number, standing before the throne and before the Lamb" (Rev 7:9a). Hispanics, Asians, African Americans, El Salvadorians, disabled persons, and women, to name a few, have a

---

[30.] McCaulley, *Reading While Black*, 22.

[31.] Anthony C. Thiselton, *New Horizons In Hermeneutics* (Grand Rapids: Zondervan, 1992), 31.

unique perspective and can share distinct emphases and insights on certain passages of Scripture.

Truth is found in the text. The reader does not establish meaning or truth; the inspired Word of God is truth. Different people from a variety of social locations find certain applications in the text that other communities might not see in a different social location. For instance, I am a disabled veteran.[32] When I read healing narratives in the Gospels, I do not lose sight of the author's meaning and intention; however, I share something similar with those in the text. Being disabled allows for a heightened awareness and insight into the biblical text that those who are not disabled do not have. Might a disabled person draw some applications from reading one of the healing narratives about how congregations can care for veterans and other disabled communities? Can an application lead congregations to help veterans or others from disabled communities navigate the complex social realities they encounter? These complexities include finding meaningful employment, facing discrimination, lack of enforcement of the American Disabilities Act, or the challenges of navigating the Affordable Care Act and other benefits these image-bearers may need to enable them to live according to God's intention and purpose. In reading John 5:1–14, might a person who suffers a debilitating injury in time of war, be able to call attention to the bureaucratic challenges that veterans face in receiving mental and physical health services after they return from war?[33] Those who come from different social locations have a lot to teach us about applying the Word of God to those who are hurting.

We should never elevate a cultural reading simply because it is cultural, nor should we jettison the foundational practices of sound biblical interpretation. We can speak more accurately to spiritual and social crises when we welcome each of our unique biblical

---

[32.] I served in the United States Navy as an active-duty sailor from August 1989–August 1993. From June 1990–August 1993, I was stationed aboard the USS Saratoga (CV-60), where we were engaged in Operation Desert Shield/Operation Desert Storm from August 7, 1990–March 28, 1991. My service-connected disability is related to those conflicts.

[33.] In 2014 the Veterans Health Administration received scrutiny over the lengthy wait times for veterans to see doctors at their facilities. Adding to the scrutiny, investigators discovered a cover-up by hospital administrators of the allegations. See, Timeline: The Arizona Republic, "The Story behind the VA Scandal," USA Today, May 21, 2014, https://www.usatoday.com/story/news/politics/2014/05/21/veterans-healthcare-scandal-shinseki-timeline/9373227/ and Mariah Blake, "Documents Show VA Debacle Began Under George W. Bush," May 30, 2014, Mother Jones, https://www.motherjones.com/politics/2014/05/veterans-affairs-backlogs-waiting-lists-george-bush/.

perspectives. This is not to suggest that the biblical text should fall into a state of relativism and subjectivity, where everyone has their own truth. Thus, it is to maintain, as McCaulley states, that we "adopt a hermeneutic of trust in which we are patient with the text in the belief that when interpreted properly it will bring a blessing and not a curse."[34] As creatures of the eternal and everlasting God, our different perspectives of his power, love, grace, and provision are told, creating a beautiful tapestry that communicates the richness of his glory and mystery.

So the goal of accepting our positive presuppositions is twofold. First, it is to realize that every reading and interpretation of Scripture has cultural and social presuppositions, some of which should be embraced by acknowledging our dependence on the Holy Spirit to act as a filter. Second, we must admit that no culture should posit their reading of the text as the dominant interpretation, or promote it as one to which others must submit. Any and all readings, theologies, and interpretations must bow to the Spirit who inspired the text, allowing for the Word of God to have the final say. In a practical sense, the sacred anthropologist should read widely from Christian scholars of minority communities, intentionally engaging in conversations with Christians from different races about how the Bible informs the church on social crises.

STEP 2: RESPECTING THE OTHER: CULTURALLY INTELLIGENT PREACHERS AND PREACHING

Steps 2 and 3 of becoming a sacred anthropologist are closely related. The Oxford Dictionary defines respect as "a feeling of deep admiration for someone or something elicited by their abilities, qualities, or achievements." Are there people whose abilities, qualities, and achievements have gone unnoticed in your life? What sources are you using to expand your knowledge in these areas? Which historical figures within communities of color do you find noteworthy as contributors to the church and society? What has your church or school taught about the history of indigenous and African American communities?

---

34. McCaulley, *Reading While Black*, 20.

Kim, in his groundbreaking book *Preaching with Cultural Intelligence: Understanding the People Who Hear Our Sermons*, has effectively argued that congregations, and most importantly preachers, need cultural intelligence. He contends that ". . . the preacher who displays cultural intelligence when preaching is simultaneously and subconsciously building bridges between and among his congregants, who often come from very dissimilar cultural contexts. Congregational cultural intelligence is a trait that is sorely missing in many churches today."[35] The most effective preachers immerse themselves in reading beyond their normal sphere of interest, cultural location, and social interactions. Since many social crises occur between warring factions, any responsible and effective attempt to leverage the gospel on these issues would require the preacher to be aware of the customs, beliefs, values, and fears of the people involved. Too often, preachers irresponsibly (and sometimes hurtfully) hurl suggestions at communal problems, of which they have no understanding, experience, or knowledge. One of the chief abilities of any preacher is to understand their listeners. Culturally intelligent preachers possess the necessary skills to help diverse congregations navigate complex social issues.

Our feelings and convictions about our neighbor are not only limited to the racially "other." They extend towards the abilities, qualities, and achievement of disabled persons, women, different denominations, other religions, socioeconomic groups, and even the elderly, groups in which respect is sometimes at a minimum. So it is only natural that Step 2, which promotes respect among our neighbors, calls for Step 3, resisting the stereotypes associated with our neighbor. To garner respect, we must remove the myths and stereotypes we associate with certain people by acquiring cultural intelligence, education, and relationships.

The sacred anthropologist should be conscious of and acquainted with the cultures of the individuals who hear our sermons week after week. As our Sunday morning worship services began to increase in ethnic and racial representation, I learned very early to discern the different ethnicities, ages, physical abilities, and even the people's opinions in the pews of Plum Grove Baptist Church. Knowing their cultural histories, convictions, former faith traditions, hurts, the communities

---

[35.] Kim, *Preaching with Cultural Intelligence*, 3.

where they were raised, along with the dynamics of their relationships, has had a profound effect on how I approach social crisis preaching. Respecting the diversity of my congregation has had a profound effect on how they respond to my messages. A sermon that promotes the beauty of marriage should not demonize single, divorced, or widowed people. If a text leads me to challenge young and healthy people to serve the Lord with gladness, the sermon should not make those who are physically disabled or elderly feel as if they have nothing to contribute. But knowing these things is only one part of this dynamic; preachers must develop the competence of cultural intelligence. Respecting the other is a Christian act because we are as Jesus commands when he says, "Love one another. Just as I have loved you, you are also to love one another" (John 13:34). When we respect others, we acknowledge the power and creativity of our loving God.

STEP 3: RESIST THE MYTHS AND STEREOTYPES: RACE, PROTEST AND RESISTANCE RHETORIC

On August 12, 2008, during the presidential election, amid a room full of Republican voters, the Republican nominee, the late Senator John McCain, in a town hall meeting in York, Pennsylvania, resisted the myths about his Democratic opponent, then-Senator Barak H. Obama. During this town hall, a man voiced his fears about an Obama presidency. The man anchored his fear in the myth that Senator Obama "cohorts with domestic terrorists." Immediately Senator McCain took the mic and said, "First of all, I want to be president of the United States, and obviously I don't want Senator Obama to be, but I have to tell you, he is a decent person and a person you do not have to be scared [of] as president of the United States."[36]

Shortly after this exchange, a woman stood and said, "I cannot trust Obama, I have read about him, and he is an Arab. . . ." Before she could finish her sentence, McCain began to shake his head in disagreement. Quickly and firmly in rebuttal, he said, "No ma'am, no ma'am,

[36.] YouTube, "McCain Counters Obama Arab Question," October 11, 2008, YouTube video, "McCain Counters Obama 'Arab' Question," AP, October 11, 2018, https://www.youtube.com/watch?v=jrnRU3ocIH4.

he is a decent family man, a citizen, that I happen to have disagreements with on fundamental issues, and that's what this campaign is all about." The crowd erupted in applause, seemingly in admiration for his honesty and agreement with his statement.[37] With those words, McCain accomplishes two of the steps in the sacred anthropologist model of pastoral leadership: he resisted the false, hurtful, and divisive stereotype and myth (Step 3) about Obama's birth and character, and he became a resource (Step 4) for others who need to be informed or corrected with the truth about their neighbor (Obama). Many would have allowed the false narratives to spread, using it for their advantage. Others would have been either too afraid or ill-equipped to share the truth about their neighbor. Not McCain.

Edmondson and Brennan correctly contend, "Truth telling and historical reflection are a powerful way we can help promote growth and the building up of one another in love."[38] Myths, stereotypes, and propaganda are in overdrive whenever social crises arise. Warring ideological parties feel the need to promote any negative narrative that may discredit those with whom they disagree and don't understand. Social crisis preachers are honest ambassadors of the Lord. Kim states

> Popular terms like "postracial America" presume that we, as Americans, have overcome racial hostilities and now live in a society of racial parity. Quite the contrary, racial and ethnic divides linger on across America. Even in our preaching ministry, we are either perpetuating prejudice with our silence or making progress toward peace, healing, and reconciliation in our churches. Many evangelical Christian leaders have been sluggish in exhibiting the ministry of reconciliation across racial and ethnic lines. As culturally intelligent preachers, it is paramount that we lead the charge in helping our congregations embrace and celebrate ethnic and cultural differences.[39]

Resisting the stereotypes about our neighbor can cause us to confront some very endearing sources, like our churches, denominational

---

[37.] *YouTube*, "McCain Counters Obama Arab Question."

[38.] Edmondson and Brennan, *Faithful Anti-Racism*, 84.

[39.] Kim, *Preaching with Cultural Intelligence*, 95.

theologies, and our past. The necessity of the sacred anthropologist, as one who acts in good faith to resist the stereotypes and myths of their neighbor, is paramount because of our need to confront the racist and flawed exegesis of our past.

Resisting Stereotypes Resulting from Flawed Exegesis in the Church

Racism in America's churches endured in some of the most blatantly racist eras in American history, namely the seventeenth to mid-twentieth centuries.[40] This was partly due to the flawed scientific and sociological scholarship that influenced theology and hermeneutical approaches to biblical reading and interpretation. Scholars and preachers who used the Bible to justify slavery and to support segregation were victims of these false readings. Euro-American pastors, evangelists, and slavehold-ers held an interpretation of Scripture that promoted the superiority of the Anglo-Saxon race and excluded other races as image-bearers of God. However, abolitionist ministers found arguments in Scripture for the destruction and cessation of the empire of slavery. Of these two opposing hermeneutics, Edmonson and Brennan comment, "How one group of Christians could believe that the Bible gives them the right to own other people or take their land and the other believe that they have the duty to set people free can be found in varying hermeneutical traditions represented in America.[41]

Among the flawed exegeses was the erroneous interpretation of Genesis 9, which gave rise to the "curse of Ham" theory.[42] The Bible, the Word of God, should be the standard by which all theories, ideologies, and theologies are measured. Therefore, flawed theories of humanity should never shape our theology. Our theology should shape our anthropology. The Bible is the light that exposes the philosophical and theological lies perpetuated by flawed anthropology. Anthropology can be extremely useful for understanding culture, but when it runs

---

[40.] These are the eras covering slavery and Jim Crow segregation.

[41.] Edmonson and Brennan, 40.

[42.] The "curse of Ham" myth (Gen 9:18–27) was used to demean and dehumanize Black people, because it purports that Noah cursed Canaan the descendent of Ham, the son of Noah. This myth suggests that Canaan is the father of the Canaanites, Cushites, Egyptians, and the people of Put; thus he is the ancestor of all people of color, particularity those of African descent, whose blackness is their curse, thereby sanctioning them to a life of perpetual servitude.

counter to an orthodox biblical anthropology, it is wrong. Cultural intelligence is counter to theological, anthropological ignorance and arrogance. Baptized in the Bible, cultural intelligence provides the social crisis preacher with the means to articulate what it means to be human, as the Lord intended.

It can be argued that America's original social sins-racism, slavery, and the social manifestations of racial superiority-flourished primarily due to profoundly flawed exegesis. Consider the insight of African American New Testament scholar Cain Hope Felder, "Indeed, even today, in such versions of Holy Scripture as *Dake's Annotated Reference Bible*, one finds at Genesis 9:18–27 a so-called great racial prophecy with the following racist hermeneutic:

> All colors and types of men came into existence after the flood. All men were white up to this point, for there was only one family line—that of Noah who was white and in the line of Christ, being mentioned in Luke 3:36 with his son Shem…. [There is a] prophecy that Shem would be a chosen race and have a peculiar relationship with God [v.26]. All divine revelation since Shem has come through his line…. [There is a] prophecy that Japheth would be the father of the great and enlarged races [v.27]. Government, Science and Art are mainly Japhethic….His descendants constitute the leading nations of civilization.[43]

Dr. R. Albert Mohler, Jr. confirms the disastrous effects of flawed exegesis upon race relations and its contribution to a social crisis as he describes the popularity of such paralyzing pronouncements: "At times, white superiority was defended by a putrid exegesis of the Bible that claimed a 'curse of Ham' as the explanation of dark skin—an argument that reflects such ignorance of Scripture and such shameful exegesis that it could only be believed by those who were looking for an argument to satisfy their prejudices."[44]

Social crisis proclamation strikes the biblical chords of ethnic

---

43. Cain Hope Felder, ed., *Stony the Road We Trod: African American Biblical Interpretation* (Minneapolis: Augsburg Fortress, 1991), 132.

44. Jarvis J. Williams and Kevin M. Jones, *Removing the Stain of Racism from the Southern Baptist Convention* (Nashville: B&H, 2017), location 765, Kindle.

uniqueness, producing beautiful notes of racial and ethnic harmony. Racism is still at the fore of our nation's (and our churches') problems. Until we develop preachers committed to resisting these stereotypes by learning the truth about the unique beauty of other races, cultures, and ethnicities, our social crises will continue to result from sincere ignorance and spiritual arrogance.

STEP 4: SERVE AS A RESOURCE FOR OTHER PEOPLE: ADVOCACY IN ACTION

As a pastor, college professor, administrator, and former human resources professional, I submit dozens of letters of recommendation for former students, church members, staff members, and colleagues. This provides me with an opportunity to vouch for, advocate for, and support friends, employees, and former students when their personal testimony about themselves is not enough. Occasionally, the recommendation and reference process goes a step further because I have the chance to speak with a potential employer over the phone. These are proud moments, as I serve as a resource for people who usually deserve the opportunity they are pursuing. Sometimes, all it takes is an honest, glowing recommendation for someone to get the job they need and desire.

Perhaps my most proud moments acting as a resource are when I have the opportunity to write or speak on behalf of people who have a less than stellar season in their past; a crime, a jail sentence, a job termination, a divorce, or some other personal issue, all of which they have long since put behind them by the restoring and redeeming grace of God. These times call for me to clear up misconceptions, provide a different perspective, share the truth, inform and educate, or act as McCain. The social crisis preacher has the unique opportunity to be a cultural resource for people and communities trying to shed not only the honest mistakes of their past but also the misconceptions about them. In this same way, the sacred anthropologist should be a resource for their church and community when slanderous things are propagated about people. If the church needs a better understanding of a situation or a neighboring community of a different ethnic persuasion, they should be able to go to their resident sacred anthropologist as a resource.

Whenever I preach, I try to use an illustration that shows God's love and favor in the lives of African Americans as they trod the stony road of suffering and oppression to run the race of courage and resolve on the highway towards freedom. Not only is God's faithfulness vividly seen in these examples, but I firmly believe that when people hear these lesser-known American histories, the "I didn't know" effect powerfully changes their perspective, opinions, attitudes, and actions in ways that make for repentance and reconciliation. At other times, if I am sermonically addressing crime, lawlessness, and sin in America's predominantly Black and brown communities, I am not only promoting personal responsibility, but I am also challenging the congregation to look deeper at the ramifications of slavery, Jim Crow, mass incarceration, communal neglect, and low job prospects as root causes of some of the dysfunction in those communities. I am offering a paradigm as a scholar, and a perspective from personal experience, that many in the pews do not have. I am not suggesting that all disparities everywhere in Black communities are the result of systemic racism. I am saying that there are disparities in America that are precisely due to systemic racism. Consider again, Washington's research on the historic systemic racism prevalent in medicine and medical research. Washington states

> In dissecting this shameful medial apartheid, an important cause is usually neglected: the history of ethically flawed medial experimentation with African Americans. Such research has played a pivotal role in forging the fear of medicine that helps perpetuate our nation's racial health gulf. Historically, African Americans have been subjected to exploitative, abusive involuntary experimentation at far higher than other ethnic groups. Thus, although the heightened African American wariness of medical research and institutions reflects a situational hypervigilance, it is neither a *baseless* fear of harm nor a fear of imaginary harms.[45]

Recalling this definition from Feagin, systemic racism is

> the unjustly gained socioeconomic resources and assets of whites, and the long-term maintenance of major socioeconomic inequalities

---

[45.] Washington, *Medical Apartheid*, 20–21 , (intro, n. 6).

across what came to be defined as a rigid color line . . . Systemic racism encompasses a broad range of white-racist dimensions: the racist ideology, attitudes, emotions, habits, actions, and institutions of whites in this society.[46]

When we understand systemic injustice, we must conclude that it has and does exist in our broken and fallen world. Sinful human individuals develop, create, and sustain unjust systems. Besides the systemic racism of slavery and Jim Crow, the "major socioeconomic inequalities" created by housing discrimination and the untold resources unrealized by generations of Black Americans is another example. Richard Rothstein calls attention to a glaring example of systemic racism that fits Feagin's definition precisely. Rothstein's research on redlining and housing discrimination reveals, "Government policies that segregated this nation were directed primarily at African American working- and middle-class two-parent families with children."[47] Another example is racial health disparities in the state of Alabama. The Department of Public Health has even affirmed that the COVID-19 pandemic has violently and disproportionately affected Black Alabamians. The Appleseed Project's research reveals, "The Department of Public Health is right: Alabamians of color, and particularly Black Alabamians, have disproportionately suffered from the health consequences of this pandemic. According to the COVID Tracking Project at the Atlantic, Black Alabamians had the highest death rate from COVID-19 at 84 per 100,000, followed by white Alabamians at 50 per 100,000 and Hispanic or Latinx at 38 per 100,000."[48] These grim statistics point to the fact, also reported by the Department of Health, that Black Alabamians live in poorer communities and have less access to healthcare. The sacred anthropologist, serving as a resource, uses data like this to push back on falsely represented arguments that either blame victims

---

[46] Feagin, *Systemic Racism*, 2 (intro, n.19).

[47] Richard Rothstein, *The Color of Law: A Forgotten History of How Our Government Segregated America* (New York: Liveright, 2017), 231.

[48] Alabama Appleseed Center for Law and Justice, "Flattened: How the COVID-19 Pandemic Knocked Financially Insecure Alabamians on Their Backs and Widened the Racial Prosperity Gap," https://www.alabamaappleseed.org/wp-content/uploads/2020/12/Alabama-Appleseed-Covid-Report-Flattened.pdf, 12.

of poverty or that propose illogical self-determination and personal responsibility answers for these almost impossible-to-overcome barriers.

I strongly affirm personal responsibility. But social programs such as voter enfranchisement legislation, equally performing schools, and even reparations, cannot replace the necessity and the biblical admonishment of personal responsibility. Yet no amount of personal responsibility can atone for 250 years of slavery, and another one hundred years of Jim Crow, in which Black Americans lacked agency, access, legal support, and economic and wealth equality. The point is, Christian proclamation should be undergirded with integrity. We help no one when we deny that systemic racism exists, just as no one is empowered when we cry "racism" when none exists.

I am also aware of the Black conservative intellectual tradition and the very valid points these scholars raise in favor of personal responsibility, family values, thrift, caution against underachievement, victimization, and excessive use of the term "wokeness."[49]

One notable conservative intellectual, John McWhorter, raises an interesting point: "We are in a time of transition, and we are a lot closer to the mountaintop than we are to 1950. There comes a point when we must ask not simply whether we are dealing with racism—of course we

---

[49.] The African American conservative intellectual tradition includes notable figures such as Booker T. Washington, founder of Tuskegee Normal and Industrial Institute, now Tuskegee University. Washington was the rival of the African American progressive thinker, W.E.B. Du Bois, who is noted to be the first African American to earn a doctorate from Harvard University, and one of the founders of the NAACP. Washington's "Atlanta Compromise" speech, delivered at the Cotton States and International Exposition on September 18, 1895, promoted personal responsibility, industrial education, and tolerance of racial segregation. The most notable line in the speech, "In all things that are purely social we can be as separate as the fingers, yet one as the hand in all things essential to mutual progress," assured whites that Blacks would not aggressively push for integration, but raise themselves to respectable positions in education, business, and economics before seeking integration. The "Atlanta Compromise" speech is one of the most heralded conservative speeches of the nineteenth century and solidified Washington as one of the most important leaders in the nineteenth century. See https://thehermitage.com/wp-content/uploads/2016/02/Booker-T-Washington_Atlanta-Compromise-Speech_1895.pdf. The speech and Washington came under harsh criticism from Du Bois in his classic, *The Souls of Black Folk* written in 1903. See Chapter III entitled "Of Mr. Booker T. Washington and Others," in W.E.B. Dubois, *The Souls of Black Folk*, (New York: The Modern Library, 1996), 43–61. The African American conservative tradition's most notable figures include: Economist Thomas Sowell, Professor of Linguistics John McWhorter, United States Supreme Court Associate Justice Clarence Thomas, Economist and Professor of Economics Glenn Loury, and Professor of Sociology Anne Wortham. For more on Black conservative thought see Christopher Alan Bracey, *Saviors or Sellouts: The Promise and Peril of Black Conservatism, from Booker T. Washington to Condoleezza Rice* (Boston: Beacon, 2019).

are—but how much."[50] Americans of every hue made selfless sacrifices that brought exponential strides in racial progress. The respected African American economist and conservative intellectual Thomas Sowell is right when he argues, "You cannot take any people, of any color, and exempt them from the requirements of civilization—including work, behavioral standards, personal responsibility and all the other basic things that the clever intelligentsia disdain—without ruinous consequences to them and to society at large."[51] Personal responsibility is a two-edged knife. Personal responsibility assumes that individuals and communities will partner with God, assume responsibility for self-inflicted damage, and speak truthfully to the ills of their communities. The other side of personal responsibility suggests that we all have a personal responsibility to "love your neighbor as yourself" (Mark 12:31) and to partner with God to bring about equity and liberation for all God's children.

Social crisis preachers, as sacred anthropologists, can serve as a resource to inform congregations of God's kept-promise to Abraham that "all the families of the earth shall be blessed" (Gen 12:3 ESV). The people in the pews should be informed of how, from the embryonic stages of the New Testament church, to the patristic era of the church fathers contending for the faith against heretics, to the tumultuous yet triumphant civil rights era, God has invited and used a kaleidoscope of cultures and ethnicities in his ongoing redemptive narrative. Pastors need to be resourceful. This will become increasingly more evident as multiethnic churches become the norm. Churches that are predominately Black or white in membership will start to reflect increasing numbers of other races and ethnicities due to the changing demographics in our nation.

A Resource for Ethnic Inclusion in God's Story

The need to correct hermeneutical malfeasance, that often led to the exclusion and erasure of non-white cultures from the Bible and

---

[50.] John McWhorter, *Losing the Race: Self-Sabotage in Black America* (New York: Perennial, 2001), 110.

[51.] Thomas Sowell, "Blame the welfare state, not racism, for poor blacks' problems," in *Penn Live, Patriot News*, January 5, 2019, accessed February 3, 2022, https://www.pennlive.com /opinion/2015/05/poor_blacks_looking_for_someon.html.

church history by Western scholars, preachers, and schools of divinity, is another means of being a resource for the church. Many churches are unaware of an African presence in the Bible and church history. J. Daniel Hays makes a significant point, "The terms Cush or Cushite appear 54 times in the Hebrew text of the Old Testament, indicating that the Cushites, an African people, played a fairly significant role in the Old Testament story."[52] However, this fact is not discussed, seen as irrelevant, or deemed insignificant in most evangelical schools and churches. Hays continues, "Scholars writing from other ethnic viewpoints are likewise joining this chorus in calling on White, male scholars, who dominate biblical scholarship, to reconsider how much their Anglo-American viewpoint might affect their approach to Scripture."[53] When preachers of every ethnicity can share with their multicultural congregations about the many nationalities and ethnicities included in redemption history, cultural appreciation becomes the dominant attitude, replacing feelings of inferiority and superiority.

Historically, scholars have not placed a sufficient emphasis on the geographical regions in which early Christianity developed and flourished. Thus, they have omitted the influence of Africa on Christianity. Hays rightly observes, "Within the context of the Black-White racial problems in the United States, it is significant to note that Black Africans from Cush/Ethiopia play an important role throughout Scripture."[54] Africa's presence is prominent in the Old Testament, but some of the most significant events and people in the New Testament are as well: Mary and Joseph's escape to Egypt (Matt 2:13–23); Simon of Cyrene's carrying the cross of Christ (Matt 27:32); the events of Pentecost (Acts 2); and the baptism of the Ethiopian eunuch (Acts 8:27) are all connected to Africa. Thomas Oden correctly observes,

> The global Christian mind has been formed out of a specific history, not out of bare-bones theoretical ideas. Much of that history occurred in Africa. Cut Africa out of the Bible and Christian memory,

---

[52.] J. Daniel Hays, *From Every People and Nation: A Biblical Theology of Race,* (Downers Grove, IL: IVP Academic, 2016), Kindle, 25.

[53.] Hays, Kindle, 240.

[54.] Hays, Kindle, 201.

and you have misplaced many pivotal scenes of salvation history. It is the story of the children of Abraham in Africa; Joseph in Africa; Moses in Africa; Mary, Joseph and Jesus in Africa; and shortly thereafter Mark and Perpetua and Athanasius and Augustine in Africa.[55]

Additionally, historians have excluded the presence and impact of early African church leaders upon Christianity. The attempt to associate these leaders with Roman identities has led students and scholars alike to disaffiliate these African church leaders from their culture and identity. David E. Wilhite rightly observes, "While most histories of Christianity include major African figures such as Cyprian and Augustine, few treat these subjects as Africans."[56] Wilhite further concludes that church fathers such as Tertullian, Cyprian, and Augustine self-identified as African and that, "Rome's colonizing presence did not eradicate the local population, nor did it erase the pre-Roman society's language and customs."[57] In erasing the African identity of early church fathers, there is the tendency to assume that people of African descent offered very little to Christianity; or there is the false notion that what Africans did offer to Christianity had no value. These factors, along with the inaccurate artistic portrayals of biblical characters with European features, have heightened the suspicions within Black and brown communities about the evangelistic and ministry efforts of some white churches.

Vincent Bantu further explains, "It is understandable that some African Americans perceive Christianity as an oppressive religion given the role Christianity has played in white hegemony in United States history."[58] These unbalanced teachings have led, in part, to the white superiority complex that is also the leading cause of the legacy of racial discrimination in the policies and laws across the United States, directly and negatively affecting the lives of people of African descent. This neglect is not only sinister but irresponsible, leading to the false claims that only European nations, or those whose identity can be

---

[55.] Thomas Oden, *How Africa Shaped the Christian Mind: Rediscovering the African Seedbed of Western Christianity* (Downers Grove, IL: InterVarsity, 2007), 14.

[56.] David E. Wilhite, *Ancient African Christianity* (London: Routledge, 2017), 3.

[57.] Wilhite, 46.

[58.] Vince L. Bantu, *A Multitude of All Peoples: Engaging Ancient Christianity's Global Identity* (Downers Grove, IL: IVP, 2020), 3.

traced to European countries, have made the most substantial contributions to the Christian faith. Bantu accurately surmises, "Church
historians would have us believe that Christianity came into Africa
and Asia from Europe when the reality is quite the opposite in several
significant respects. Christianity is not becoming a global religion; it
has always been a global religion."[59]

Social crisis preaching can correct these misleading narratives by
drawing from the many texts in the Bible where there are positive references to African places and people. These factors are critical, because
the most sensitive and controversial social crises that the preacher as
sacred anthropologist will have to tackle, involve issues surrounding race and racism. The proliferation of cultural superiority in the
United States is primarily due to the myths and narratives that cast
America as God's chosen nation and white European settlers as God's
chosen people. Concepts such as manifest destiny and American ex-
ceptionalism conveyed the idea that the oftentimes forcible expansion
of the United States during the mid-1800s was divinely ordained and
that America is superior to other nations, is not only taught by well-
respected Christian scholars, but is being proclaimed from pulpits.

Despite the forced displacement of millions of indigenous people
from their native land, and the fact that African slavery was in full
effect, sermons like John Winthrop's "City on a Hill" promoted the
idea that America, despite these crimes of humanity, is exceptional.
God's promise to Abraham includes all nations. Whether the country is
America, Japan, Iraq, or England, "righteousness exalts a nation, but sin
is a disgrace to any people" (Prov 14:34). Preachers must proclaim the
superiority of God and the inferiority of all people before his presence.

A Resource for Changing Demographics

Another reason the church needs social crisis preachers who are a resource to their church and communities, is to better communicate and
understand the changing demographics in the country and the church.
E. Randolph Richards and Brandon J. O'Brien comment, "Many
sociologists estimate that by 2050, the majority of US citizens will be

---

[59] Bantu, *A Multitude of All People*, 2.

nonwhite. Demographic changes in the United States population in general are changing the face of Christianity in the US."[60] US census results indicate that the racial and ethnic composition of America is changing. Two factors are contributing to these shifting demographics. First, according to the US Census Bureau, "The non-Hispanic White population is projected to shrink over coming decades, from 199 million in 2020 to 179 million people in 2060—even as the US population continues to grow. Their decline is driven by falling birth rates and rising number of deaths over time as the non-Hispanic White population ages."[61] Second, as the Census Bureau states, "The population of people who are Two or More Races is projected to be the fastest-growing racial or ethnic group over the next several decades, followed by Asians and Hispanics."[62]

These changing demographics mean changing interests, translating into competing ideological issues that create social crises. According to the Pew Research Center, "The number of eligible voters who are Hispanic (32 million) is projected to surpass that of eligible black voters (30 million) for the first time."[63] The leading cause of these shifting demographics is the increase of people from other nations seeking refuge or relocation in the United States. One of the most controversial crises in American history and our current political context is that of immigration. The leading voices on these matters must come from the church. Despite where one stands on immigration, the sacred anthropologist is responsible for teaching that all people, regardless of their land of origin, are created in the image of God. Likewise, as the country in which we live changes, the church will change in its cultural and ethnic makeup. As a result, the concerns of our congregations will expand to focus on the social crises confronting us, regardless of our race, sex, religion, or socioeconomic context. As we see in the

[60]. E. Randolph Richards and Brandon J. O'Brien, *Misreading Scripture with Western Eyes: Removing the Cultural Blinders to Better Understand The Bible*, (Downers Grove, IL: IVP, 2012), 17.

[61]. Jonathan Vespa, Lauren Medina, and David M. Armstrong, "Demographic Turning Points for the United States: Population Projections for 2020 to 2060," February 2020, https://www.census.gov/content/dam/Census/library/publications/2020/demo/p25-1144.pdf.

[62]. Vespa, Medina, and Armstrong

[63]. Anthony Ciluffo and D'Vera Cohn, "6 Demographic Trends Shaping the U.S. and the World in 2019," April 2019, *Pew Research Center*, https://www.pewresearch.org/fact-tank/2019/04/11/6-demographic-trends-shaping-the-u-s-and-the-world-in-2019/.

current COVID-19 crisis, the preacher must educate, inform, and be the voice of reason within a world that is divided on almost every issue imaginable. The sacred anthropologist must serve as a resource for all people and all things.

STEP 5: A CALLING FOR AN INTENTIONAL RESPONSE: CONGREGATIONAL CARE

At the time of this writing, President Joe Biden has signed legislation making Juneteenth a federal holiday, after decades of pleading from African American groups and individuals like Opal Lee to do so.[64] Lee, considered the grandmother of Juneteenth, 89 years old at the time, started a lone march to Washington, DC, in 2016 to ask then-President Barak Obama to make Juneteenth a holiday. Although Juneteenth did not become a holiday under President Obama's tenure, Lee's commitment to bring awareness to the holiday was just beginning. She did not complete the 1,400–mile trek from her native Texas to Washington, DC. Instead, she started a personal tradition of walking 2.5 miles every Juneteenth, for the purpose of raising awareness and attention to the day, where on June 19, 1865, Major General Gordon Granger issued General Order No. 3 that informed enslaved persons in Galveston, Texas, that they were free from the dehumanizing, nightmarish ordeal of chattel slavery.[65] In December of that same year, the 13th Amendment was ratified, forever abolishing slavery in the United States and its territories.

Immediately after the news broke about the new holiday, sentiments varied from celebration and thanksgiving, to indifference and apathy, to bitter objection. Simultaneously, major department store chains and other commercial enterprises started to advertise "Juneteenth sales," raising the ire of many. Since most African American communities and churches had a history of celebrating Juneteenth, the reaction to the national holiday news was viewed as a win in the long contest for progress in creating more awareness about African Americans' unique

---

[64.] Annie Karni and Luke Broadwater, "Biden Signs Law Making Juneteenth a Federal Holiday," June 19, 2021, *The New York Times*, https://www.nytimes.com/2021/06/17/us/politics/juneteenth-holiday-biden.html.

[65.] Katie Kindelan, "Meet Opal Lee, the grandmother of the movement to make Juneteenth a federal holiday," *ABC News* via *GMA*, June 18, 2021, https://abcnews.go.com/GMA/News/meet-opal-lee-grandmother-movement-make-juneteenth-federal/story?id=78356537.

struggles. But the glaring questions became, "How would white Americans celebrate Juneteenth?" or, "Should they celebrate this monumental day?" when many had not even heard of it. Others "felt some kind of way"; still others were happy for the posterity of the people freed on that glorious day 156 years ago. For me, the answer came through a student's sermon preached on June 19, 2021, during a doctor of ministry "Text to Sermon Preaching Seminar" I was co-teaching at Beeson Divinity School with Smith, Jr.

Dustin Jernigan's sermon from Esth 9:20–28 was entitled "Hors D'Oeuvres to the Feast."[66] In his introduction, he related the origins of Juneteenth and the news of the legislation that led to it becoming a national holiday. This was a reason, even for people in his hometown of Jacksonville, Oregon, with its 97 percent white population, to rejoice in the goodness of God and his saving actions towards those he loves.

Jernigan eloquently told the story of King Ahasuerus and his lavish six-month party, seven-day feast of drunkenness, and his exploitation of women and girls, Esther being one of them. He then moves to Haman's murderous plot to destroy the Jews, Mordecai's petition to Esther to intervene from her place of privilege, and Esther's brilliant plan to throw a feast to reveal her identity as a Jew, where the concocted plan of Haman was foiled. As a result of Haman being exposed, and consequently sentenced to death, and the Jews being delivered, Esther and Mordecai reflect on this mighty deliverance (and most likely Yahweh, though he is not explicitly mentioned). In their reflection, they imagine a feast in which to celebrate, and they invite everyone!

Then Jernigan provides sermonic commentary about how on the fourteenth day of the month of Adar, the Jewish holiday and feast of Purim was instituted, "not based on mere human enjoyment, but human joy in God's greatness and character." He boldly proclaims, "Friends, is this not a message for us today? The deliverance that today's holiday commemorates, is it not a reason for the African American community to deeply rejoice? But is it not also a testimony to our nation, to our world, that God is a God who delivers, who hears the cry of the oppressed, and can redeem any situation?"

[66.] Dustin Jernigan, "Hors D'Oeuvres to the Feast," Esther 9:20–28, Seminar, "Text to Sermon Preaching," Beeson Divinity School, Birmingham, AL, June 19, 2021. Dustin Jernigan is the pastor of Jacksonville Presbyterian Church in Jacksonville, Oregon.

The sermonic application of Jernigan's message was that "we as Christians are free to celebrate and rejoice in this life through holidays and celebrations, including today, but only when we celebrate with an eye towards the final holiday, the ultimate celebration: the return of Christ, all holidays are simply hors d'oeuvres to the wedding feast at the end of time, the marriage supper of the Lamb."

Lament as a Congregational Response to Crises

The book of Esther provides some clues as to how the social crisis preacher as sacred anthropologist calls for a response to social crises from the congregation. We must challenge people to lament social crises in our neighbor's community. In Esther chapter 4, Mordecai "tore his clothes and put on sackcloth and ashes, and went out into the midst of the city, and he cried out with a loud and bitter cry" (Esth 4:1b ESV). Esther's compassionate response to Mordecai's lament represents the kind of empathy that should accompany a Christian's consciousness. When injustice abounds, regardless of whom it affects, there should be a spiritual sensitivity within us that causes our hearts to break. Biblically, to lament is to complain, to cry out to God, to sorrow. It is usually associated with an individual or a communal crisis. Lament is a valid, ordained response, directed in confidence to a personal, sovereign, and loving God. In lament, we petition God for help while expressing trust, thanksgiving, and a willingness to wait (Pss 44, 74, 90).

In Esth 9:31, Esther instructs future Jews about the appropriate way to observe Purim: with fasting and lamentation preceding and accompanying celebration. Esther and Mordecai knew the sorrow that made the celebration sweet. These instructions were put in place so that "these days of Purim should never fall into disuse among the Jews, nor should the commemoration of these days cease among their descendants" (Esth 9:28b ESV). It is in remembering the causes of lament that we stay spiritually grounded, keeping our celebrations pure from the encroaching distractions that seek to hijack our holy days from the depths of their original meaning and remembrance. Purim is about more than celebration. The celebration must always be placed in context: Purim is also about remembering the calamities and atrocities that caused lamentation, and the exchange of beauty for ashes (Isa 61:3). The observance of Purim reminds Jews of pain as well as joy. To remember the pain helps us to do all we can to keep from revisiting the same troubles. We can learn much from Esther's and Mordecai's instructions.

Often, we want the painless experience of racial reconciliation without participating in the painful nadir of an exercise in memory. Imagine if we had to remember the atrocities of what led to the Emancipation Proclamation and Juneteenth before we sang songs, lit fireworks, hung flags, fired up barbecue grills, danced, or traveled to our beachfront condos. What if we took a few days to lament slavery or lynching, or to imagine how it must have felt for mothers to have their children snatched from their arms the moment they took their first breath? What if we tried to imagine what bondage felt like, or what it may have been like to work an entire life, never to receive remuneration or compensation? What if we took forty-eight hours before the fireworks light up the night, to sit in the dark, remembering the dark years after slavery, when the descendants of those formerly bound were attempting to pull themselves up by the bootstraps they had to make?

If we took time to lament as we remember the deliverance, we might be able to save our freedom celebrations from joyless commercialism and the thoughtless antics that often accompany them. Our celebrations will be much more meaningful if we reflect on the pain before the celebration, because we will be more resolved to not relive the pain that required God's deliverance. Sacred anthropologists should lead congregations to respond to social crises through lament. In this role, social crisis preachers must challenge churches and communities to "weep with those who weep" (Rom 12:15).

Interruption as a Congregational Response for the Masses

Both Esther and Mordecai took the unselfish risk to save the Jewish people. Esther chose to make the Jews' problem her problem (Esth 7:3–4). One could argue that Mordecai could have asked Esther to save him alone, since she "obeyed Mordecai just as when she was brought up by him" (2:20b ESV). He could have benefited as an associate of the privileged Queen Esther; however, he chose to associate himself with the masses. Thurman soberly reminds us, "the masses of men live with their backs constantly against the wall. They are the poor, the disinherited, the dispossessed. What does our religion say to them?"[67]

Together Mordecai and Esther chose to disrupt an established custom and law for the sake of the most vulnerable (Esth 4–8). Often, we are taught to read Esther's interruptive actions as an act against the evil Haman. We tend to see this narrative as good versus evil. We separate Haman, the evil man, from Haman, the government authority—worthy of obedience and allegiance. But we cannot forget that Esther's actions were against the established government of King Ahasuerus; ultimately, it was he and his law that Esther defied. It was the king who promoted Haman (3:1); gave him authority as a government representative (3:2); gave Haman his signet ring (3:10); and had his scribes write the edict making Haman's bill of legislation a law to be enforced in all the king's provinces (3:12–14). But decrees and laws can be morally wrong, especially when they are constructed and devised by evil people to be used as weapons against a particular group of people. In this case, they must be defied, and the systems and processes that allow immoral laws and policies to flourish must be creatively and courageously interrupted. On more than one occasion, Esther's actions interrupted the powerful flow of flawed legislation and ultimately led to the repeal of a destructive law (8:3–12).

Challenging congregations to intentionally care about and confront the crises in their neighbor's community by calling them to interrupt the injustices that affect the masses is a form of public Christianity. It begs us to ask the question, "What kind of public witness do I bear that will positively affect the masses of vulnerable people?" Sally A. Brown poignantly points to Christians as "agents of redemptive interruption."[68] Brown states, "Preachers become 'agents of [redemptive] interruption' when they question or unmask the fear that lurks behind the swaggering threats of the powers of this world."[69]

Affluent and privileged Black and white congregations, who have similar socioeconomic congregational makeups, cannot afford to leave

---

[67]. Howard Thurman, *Jesus and the Disinherited* (Boston: Beacon, 1976), 12.

[68]. Sally A. Brown, *Sunday's Sermon for Monday's World*, 54 (intro, n. 24).

[69]. Brown, 55.

behind the masses of people who are yet in the throes of racial discord. Like Mordecai and Esther, they must make the problems of the masses their problems. Racial reconciliation cannot become the religious rhetoric that they define as pulpit swaps, prayer meetings, and block parties, while at the same time, they avoid tackling the crippling conditions that make inner cities cesspools of violence, drugs, and promiscuity, in which the masses wade every day. Congregations must interrupt the habits, systems, and policies that continue to perpetuate pockets of communal despair.

CONCLUSION

The sacred anthropologist is the pastor who is culturally aware, spiritually alive, and endeavors to know the people who listen to the Word of God as it is proclaimed. The sacred anthropologist is a model for pastoral ministry, worthy of adopting in our current times of social crises, political turmoil, and ecclesiastical divisiveness. When social crisis preachers become a culturally intelligent exegete of Scripture and people, congregational effectiveness ensues. The first step in this process begins with social crisis preachers **recognizing** their own presuppositions concerning the biblical text and the people in the pews. Doing so will lead to a greater sense of **respect** for our neighbor's culture and community, as we work to **resist** any dehumanizing, false, and unproductive myths and stereotypes about them. As we take gallant steps to become a **resource** of truth on our neighbor's behalf, we will also serve as the catalyst to challenge our congregations to **respond** with lament and the creative act of interrupting the social crises that afflict our neighbors.

CHAPTER 3:

DESIGNING THE SERMON

Theological Function and Social Crisis Focus

HOMILETICAL APPROACH AND METHODOLOGY

In my definition, I contend that social crisis preaching is "biblically rooted, Spirit-enabled proclamation that develops and drives congregations to compassionately care for and radically confront social crises in the communities where their neighbors live, work, worship, and play." In this chapter I introduce the social crisis sermon template, a helpful tool that enables preachers to deliver sermons addressing social crises from the Bible with integrity. This template is a guide that will provide theological functionality and social crisis focus to the sermon. Human life can never be divorced from theology. Like a collision-avoidance system in a new vehicle alerts drivers when they are in danger of veering off the road, the social crisis sermon template will alert preachers when they are veering off into the rough shoulder of irrelevant proclamation onto the median of compromising political speech. This template is designed to keep the Word of God at the center of the social crisis sermon.

Preachers effectively fulfill this definition of social crisis preaching as defined in this book by employing homiletical strategies. Although this definition is favorable to pastors, since they are given the sacred responsibility, under the superintending presence of the Spirit, to make disciples, provide spiritual formation, and communicate God's Word to his people, it is not limited to pastors. Itinerant preachers, seminary students, youth leaders, associate pastors, visiting ministers, and any preacher who loves humanity and is sensitive to the social crises that mar God's intended purpose for his people, can do social crisis preaching.

Social crisis sermons should have both a theological and a social crisis function. To be clear, sermons ought to articulate a robust Christian theology deeply rooted within the history, creeds, and confessions of the church for the past two millennia. Drawing from this long tradition, sermons stir faith communities to know God and to act wisely and winsomely in their everyday contexts. To state differently, social crisis preaching functions theologically to exhort, make disciples, teach, and instruct in the Christian faith. It faithfully heralds biblical texts that speak of social action, while also inspiring the people of God towards social action. Social crisis preaching affirms that the Scriptures do not merely describe crises in an ancient world; they also awaken congregations and prescribe how they might care about and confront their present social crises. This conversation leads to the second point concerning a homiletical approach to social crisis preaching.

Social crisis sermons should by default focus on social crises. To repeat, I define a social crisis as "biblically rooted, Spirit-enabled proclamation that develops and drives congregations to compassionately care for and radically confront social crises in the communities where their neighbors live, work, worship, and play." My definition locates social crisis preaching within the area of Christian proclamation. This focus anchors the social crisis sermon to theological functions so that the winds of social and political agendas do not cause the sermon to drift into the realms of secular speech. It functions theologically to exhort, teach, make disciples, and instruct in the Christian faith, edifying the body of Christ. The social crisis sermon must maintain biblical integrity so that the potency of the Word of God and sound theology becomes the catalyst for social change. And sound theology is lived out in our social relationships.

The focus of the social crisis sermon aims at addressing a particular social crisis. A social crisis is a disordered condition within a community that disrupts people's *shalom* (peace) and flourishing. Veronica Squires further explains

The conditions of our neighborhood, our jobs, our education, and the social structures surrounding us have a direct impact on health status and life expectancy. People who live in disadvantaged neighborhoods are more likely to have a heart attack than people who live in middle-class neighborhoods, even when income is taken into account. If social determinants such as poverty, education, living environments, and social status are contributing to disease, what are we going to do about it?[1]

Joseph Jeter refers to this focus as "naming the monster." He comments, "To name the monsters that terrify our people is both to assure our people that we appreciate the gravity of the situation and also to lay the groundwork for understanding it."[2] A social crisis sermon avoids vague, nonspecific, ambiguous purposes that often leave parishioners confused about what the preacher sought to accomplish. Sermons that are not specific in focus may inspire but leave hearers uncommitted in their response and application.

A sermon that aims to address the dehumanizing and death-dealing social crisis of gun violence in cities throughout the United States must not merely be reduced to messages on peace. The preacher must "name the monster" of gun violence. Peace may be the end goal, but unless the preacher gives a specific name to why there is no peace, the hearers could leave without considering their positions on permitless carry or stricter gun laws, relative to the alternative vision God offers his people. The social crisis sermon cannot "beat around the bush." It must be the burning bush that commissions congregations to take action, leading them to care about and confront the social crisis in their neighbor's community in the power of the Holy Spirit. The theological function and social focus of the sermon are distilled in the social crisis template.

SOCIAL CRISIS SERMON TEMPLATE INTRODUCTION

The template below ensures that the sermon has the necessary aspects to make the sermon effective and powerful. It includes thirteen components that will maintain the theological functionality and social

---

[1] Veronica Squires and Breanna Lathrop, *How Neighborhoods Make Us Sick: Restoring Health and Wellness to Our Communities* (Downers Grove, IL: IVP, 2019), 23.
[2] Joseph R. Jeter, Jr., *Crisis Preaching: Personal & Public* (Nashville: Abingdon, 1998), 79.

crisis focus in the sermon. I will list the terms and provide probing questions the preacher should ask when preparing the social crisis sermon. Then I will define each component and conclude with a sermonic demonstration of each element from my social crisis sermon, "The Myth of More," based on Luke 12:13–34.

SOCIAL CRISIS SERMON TEMPLATE

Preaching Text: What is the preaching text? Why did you choose it? What presuppositions do you have in approaching the text? How would other interpretive communities read and interpret this text? What can you glean from them to help in your blind spots?

Title: Does the title hint at or tease the listener as to the main thought of the pericope? Is it memorable? Attractive?

Genre: What is the genre? Is there a subgenre in the preaching passage? What preaching considerations are produced by the genre of the pericope?

Social Crisis Sermon Statement (SCSS): In one sentence, how does this sermon address a current social crisis? This must be a SOUND statement: Short, Obvious, Uniting the theology of the text to the contemporary crisis, the Nucleus (the center or core of the sermon), Deliberate.

Biblical Background: What cultural, social, or economic considerations are in the text? What is the setting of the author? What's going on politically at the time of the writing of this text? Who are the powerful characters in the text? Who are the exploited? What social conditions produced the writing of the text?

Theological Relevance: Is there a particular doctrine that addresses this social crisis? Is there a major theme of the Bible, such as creation, redemption, or justice, that informs how we should view and respond to this social crisis? Why should the church be concerned about this matter? What is the Christian position(s) on this social crisis? What has the church taught about this social crisis?

Contemporary Social Crisis: What social crisis will this sermon confront? How does this crisis affect your neighbor and your neighbor's community? How much do you know about this crisis? How have you and/or your congregation been involved? What pre-proclamation functions have you engaged in? This is usually expressed in the Social Crisis Sermon Statement.

Concerns for Hearer: How well do you know this congregation? Are you aware of their knowledge of this crisis? How has it affected this congregation's community? What convictions, fears, and beliefs does this congregation hold about this crisis? Will the sermon be inductive or deductive?

Interdisciplinary Content: What data will you use to support the thrust of this sermon? Are there statistics available to support your points? How will they be used? Are there any historical lessons or data to support the sermon's main points and subpoints? What are the sources and/or authority from which the interdisciplinary content will come? Are these sources biased?

Theologically Comprehensible Language: Which theological terms in the text require an explanation? What illustrations or metaphors will you use to make the theological language or doctrine comprehensible? Is there a doctrine or theological teaching that needs to be explained to the congregation? What position has the church taken concerning this crisis? Has the church been silent on this crisis? Has the church been complicit in this crisis?

Courage: What does the sermon challenge you as a preacher to confront? Will there be resistance and opposition to this sermon (see concerns for the hearer)?

Redemptive Takeaway: What is the hope of Christ concerning this crisis? How does the Word of God speak to this crisis?

Fulfillment of SCSS: How does this sermon help to develop congregations to intentionally care about and confront the social crises in their neighbor's community in the power of the Holy Spirit? What is the application? What does the sermon call the Christian and the congregation to do?

UNDERSTANDING THE TERMS IN THE TEMPLATE

The Preaching Text

The previous chapter dealt with text selection and gave examples of how preachers can move from text to sermon through cues and clues in the Bible. Selecting the correct text enables the preacher as exegete to locate the social crisis in the text and then address it in their neighbor's community. Text selection is a sacred partnership between the preacher and the Spirit who inspired the text. The sermonic event begins when the preacher is gripped by and encounters the triune God in the text. The preacher not only selects the text, but the text selects the preacher.

There have been countless times when a sermon idea came to mind, and I selected a text to preach, but after wrestling and sitting with the text, there remained a restlessness and an unsettled feeling. It was not until I yielded to the Holy Spirit's guidance, direction, and urging that another text selected me, and the sermon preparation commenced. The evidence is not only a feeling of peace but an experience of being consumed, captivated, and unable to escape the revelations the Holy Spirit is revealing in the text for that specific preaching moment. As a seminary student at Beeson Divinity School, my preaching professor, Smith, Jr., urged us to read our preaching passage fifty times before beginning any exegetical study or formulating any part of the sermon. In doing so, the preacher enters the world of the text, and the text enters the spirit and being of the preacher. Today, I read my selected passage dozens of times slowly, meditatively, and prayerfully to hear what the Spirit is saying through the text.

The text should be announced, read sacredly in the tone and tenor for which it calls. Nothing is less convincing than a dry, monotone, emotionless reading of Scripture. The preaching text should encapsulate as many verses as necessary to give the congregation its context. Kuruvilla refers to the preaching text as pericopes. He defines the pericope as that which "refers to a portion of the biblical text that is of manageable size for homiletical and liturgical use in an ecclesial setting."[3] Preachers should avoid preaching single verses. They should consider the thought divisions of the biblical author instead of chapters and verse divisions. The author's thought can span chapters—begin in one chapter and end in the next. For instance, the household codes in Ephesians start at 5:21 and end at 6:9. Preachers must consider reading the complete thought for context. The announcement and reading of the text are the first signals that the rhetoric going forth is sacred and has the potency to remedy the social ills it is about to address.

Whenever the Scriptures are read publicly, biblical literacy increases, and the Word of God is elevated, as the bread on which the body of Christ lives. Kuruvilla also suggests, "it is through pericopes, read and exposited in congregations as fundamental units of the scriptural text, that the community of God corporately encounters the Bible."[4] When social crisis preaching centers on the biblical text as the sermon's source, the community is being formed, beginning the development of congregations that care about and confront the social crisis in their neighbor's community.

Title

The sermon title should reflect or hint at what the sermon is about. In literary terms, this is called foreshadowing. I prefer short titles, typically no more than five words, because shorter titles are easier for the hearer to remember. In addition, I find it effective to announce the title throughout the sermon. In the sermon template above, I told the title in a run,[5] with rhetorical rhythm, to emphasize how the "myth of more" is a harmful mantra to live by.

[3.] Abraham Kuruvilla, *Privilege the Text*, 91 (ch. 2, n. 41).

[4.] Kuruvilla, 91.

[5.] A run is a rhetorical scheme, whereby the preacher exhorts the congregation with statements that have a similar sound or that carry a similar meaning to drive home a point of the sermon. The statements are made in a consecutive, back-to-back manner, in an up-tempo, elevated tone of voice for rhetorical effect.

Sermon Excerpt (from Luke 12:13–34): The myth of more is deceptive because man cannot live by bread alone. **The myth of more** is draining because it requires "more" time, energy, and attention than one can give. **The myth of more** is dissatisfying because you are never satisfied. **The myth of more** is denial that God is enough and grace is sufficient!

In the call and response tradition, this often proves effective in stirring the heart and stimulating the congregation's mind. The preacher should never sacrifice the title's function to identify the topic for style, or to impress the congregation with flowery but meaningless words. But there are times when the preacher can both capture what the sermon is about and arrest the hearer's attention simultaneously.

Some of my sermon titles and texts are listed in examples below. The preacher can often create captivating titles by using literary devices such as alliteration. Some examples of sermon titles I have used are: "Lessons from a Lad," from John 6:1–14 and "A Cry in Crisis," from Jeremiah 8. The goal of having an arresting title is not merely to appear clever. Instead, it is to provide a foretaste of the substance of the sermon to come, leaving the hearer with a sweet aftertaste that reminds them that "man must not live on bread alone but on every word that comes from the mouth of God" (Matt 4:4).

Sometimes a play on words in the form of a paradoxical phrase like, "Dark Days and Bright Night," from 2 Cor 4:7–18, or "the Facts of our Faith," from Jas 1:2–12, can spark interest immediately. Simplicity is another safe, but very effective way to produce a sermon title. For instance, "Do Not Commit Adultery" from Matt 5:27–30, and, "Do Not Judge," from Matthew 7 use a direct, straightforward approach that listeners appreciate. There are times when preachers can borrow the title of a very familiar song or movie. When this is done, they should select a movie with which the congregation is familiar. I have used this strategy in sermons like "The Designated Survivor" from Jonah 1, or "Tales from the Crypt" from Mark 16:1–8, or "Their Eyes Were Watching God" from Psalm 123. The genius of this strategy (and sometimes the challenge) is that it almost automatically makes for a very memorable and vivid illustration for the introduction of the sermon.

Genre

Identifying the biblical genre is paramount in any form of preaching; this provides an insightful approach to the text. The text's genre will determine the hermeneutical approach and the preaching strategy. An Old Testament narrative requires storytelling and will often be an inductive sermon type. Thomas Long provides valuable wisdom for preachers who preach from the prophets:

> Preaching from the prophetic literature involves the preacher in two broad tasks: (1) viewing life through the lens of God's covenant and imaginatively proclaiming the vision of human society, both in personal and social dimensions, living in responsiveness and obedience to God; and (2) truthfully and courageously naming the discrepancies between this vision and the way people are presently living.[6]

Preaching a social crisis sermon from the epistles demands that the preacher focuses on the historical context and cultural circumstances particular to the letter. Scott Hafemann wisely contends, "The theology presented in the Epistles is a theology which is not only expressed in terms of a specific historical context, but which also comes to expression precisely because of that context and is expressed in application to that context."[7]

Preaching from the book of Proverbs requires a unique approach in interpretation and delivery. Proverbs are not promises. They are godly principles for living that generally hold true. The proverb, "The reward for humility and fear of the LORD is riches and honor and life" (Prov 22:4 ESV), does not mean that humble and godly people will be wealthy and problem-free. When preaching social crisis sermons from Proverbs, preachers should bring the teachings of the entire canon alongside, or even in contrast, with the principle in the Proverbs. Preaching the social crisis sermon from Proverbs invites

---

6. Thomas G. Long, "Preaching from the Prophets," in *Handbook of Contemporary Preaching*, ed. Michael Duduit (Nashville: B&H, 1992), 309.

7. Scott Hafemann, "Preaching in the Epistles," in *Handbook of Contemporary Preaching*, ed. Michael Duduit (Nashville: B&H, 1992), 309.

opportunities to preach topical or thematic sermons. In this way, an integrated approach to the theme or topic is treated through various Scriptures throughout the Bible. Preachers must caution themselves not to cherry-pick biblical text to build a personal agenda or support a flawed presupposition.

Social crisis sermons preached from the Psalms are abundant, because there are many texts concerning justice (Pss 109:2–3; 140:1–2, 12–13) and God's concern for the poor (Pss 12:5; 35:9–10; 113:5–8). But the poetry and prayers in many of the Psalms deserve attention. For instance, Ps 103:3 that says, "He forgives all your iniquity; he heals all your diseases," should not be preached as a promise that God will heal all the diseases of those who are ill and without healthcare. But the genre informs us that this song is the writer's worship to God, meant to express the power, might, and far reaches of God's blessings within his sovereign will and purpose.

Social Crisis Sermon Statement (SCSS)

The SCSS is one sentence that sums up the social crisis sermon. Much like J. H. Jowett, who said, "no sermon is ready for preaching, not ready for writing out, until we can express its theme in a short, pregnant sentence as clear as crystal,"[8] I contend that the social crisis sermon statement should be a SOUND statement containing five essential elements.

First, it should be **short**. The social crisis sermon statement should be brief enough for the preacher and the congregation to remember. If possible, it should be constructed without use of the word "and." The SCSS keeps the preacher focused, to help avoid the temptation of wading into other social crises the sermon will not allow adequate time to address.

Second, the relationship between the text and the title should be **obvious**. If asked, the SCSS should make sense the first time people hear it and need no explanation. The statement should not cause hearers to side-eye and question its relevance to the text or sermon title.

[8.] J. H. Jowett, *The Preacher, His Life, and Work,* Light By Design, Lecture IV, Location 803, Kindle.

Third, it should **unite** the theology of the text to the contemporary social crisis it is addressing. Social crises always pose theological questions. If the preacher fails to make the connection between the theology of the text and the social crisis, there can hardly be a Christian prescription to the crises being addressed. In the sermon below, my SCSS is, "Wherever greed and covetousness exist, it is a sign that we have a self-centered outlook, which hinders us from looking out for others."

Fourth, the SCSS should be the **nucleus** or the center, out of which all the sermonic points and subpoints flow. The SCSS prevents the sermon from being about three or four different issues. I chose to address the crisis of how greed is ultimately a disregard for the poor. The wealth gap (that I show through interdisciplinary content) is ever-widening. In the twenty-first century, ghettos, poor schools, substandard healthcare, and poverty exist in Earth's wealthiest nation.

Fifth, the SCSS should be **deliberate**. It should be constructed meditatively and prayerfully. Deliberation will keep the SCSS from becoming general and boring, and it also allows for creativity. My original statement was, "Greed and covetousness are not markers of balancing checkbooks, but rather an imbalance in our souls reflected in how we treat the have-nots." This original statement is accurate and creative, since it plays on "balance" and "imbalance" (showing that the root of social crises are spiritual crises, as seen Luke 12:20). But the second statement better encompasses the whole of the preaching text and the contemporary social crisis. It deals with the whole notion of how our outlook, worldviews, and life principles, though sincere, can easily slide into secular philosophical mantras that produce structures, systems, and laws that don't reflect God's concern for the poor. This deliberate development of the SCSS allows for the creative play on the words "outlook" and "look out." Christian philosophies (outlook) promote Christian practices (looking out for one's neighbor).

Biblical Background

Social crisis preachers should be textual investigative detectives who leave no stone unturned in the hermeneutical search for meaning and significance. The biblical background is often neglected during the exegetical process. Biblical writers provide clues of significance if we are willing to ask questions about the author's cultural context, socioeconomic status, customs in which they write, and the reasons for which they are writing.

The world behind the text is worth being explored as the preacher moves to preach the world in front of the text. The biblical background of the text should challenge the preacher to engage the text and asks specific questions concerning the political, economic, and social conditions of the author and original readers. The answers to these questions provide clues to the purpose in which the text was written to address. We should also raise questions about the author's reasons for using unique or rare words in the written text. In the "Myth of More," I investigate why Jesus is teaching about greed and anxiety. I consider the socioeconomic status of those being taught, namely the disciples, as evidence that anyone can be tempted by greed.

Additionally, in this sermon, I asked questions about inheritance customs, about which the author is clearly familiar. Could this custom be manipulated or abused by the brother who has possession of the inheritance? Obviously, there is a problem, because Jesus is asked to intervene. Preachers cannot be quick just to accept traditional teachings of parables because they fit nicely into their denominations' or traditions' understanding of that text. While traditional teaching on this text aims to criticize the brother who asked Jesus to intervene, I am more prone to come to his defense as a possible victim of an exploited custom.

It is clear the brother feels that he is being wronged. Jesus does not condemn him as a manipulator but instead challenges both brothers in 12:15 ("he said to them . . .") to consider their motives and possible greed. This leads me to raise questions about any custom or system that withholds goods, services, and resources that other people should have a right to. Like this dispute between brothers, sometimes good systems and customs can be manipulated to the point that they create hierarchal relationships, where power is leveraged against the weak when we are supposed to be brothers. My exegetical argument is that the parable of the rich fool is for both brothers to consider, not just one. But these questions come from investigating the background of the text.

Contemporary Social Crisis

What social crisis will the sermon confront? Preachers should not make every concern a social crisis. It is here that we must return to what constitutes a social concern. Allen writes

> I consider a social issue to have the following characteristics. It is public. People are aware of it, or should be aware of it. The issue affects the community as a community, that is, it creates social consequences. It affects the well-being of the society. Many social issues are systemic. Social issues may call for the community to invoke a common understanding or behavior in light of the issue.[9]

Public crises that adversely affect people's lives, and of which people should be aware, is why social crisis preaching is a call for pastors to develop congregations to care about and confront the social crises in their neighbor's community. Social crises are major ordeals in the lives of people and communities. Buttrick provides a criterion where he qualifies the concerns deserving of pulpit attention. He declares, "To be addressed by preaching, a situation ought to connect with profound ontological or historical questions."[10] Many crises have historical roots that have caused historical trauma; these are ongoing problems that require political, financial, social, and spiritual solutions. An example of a profound ontological question might be, "How does the legalization of marijuana pose ethical and moral dilemmas for those who are currently incarcerated for its use and/or sale and distribution?" An additional ontological question may be, "How might the legalization of gambling pose serious ethical problems for poor families who live in states with substandard high school and college performance scores?" These are serious contemporary public concerns that adversely affect the people we love and serve.

Buttrick gives another reason deserving of note, by stating that "a situation ought to fit into structures of Christian consciousness."[11] Some situations appear to be acceptable and embraced by most of the

9. Allen, "Preaching on Social Issues," 59 (see intro, n. 11).
10. Buttrick, *Homiletic*, 425 (see chap. 1, n. 22).
11. Buttrick, 425.

mainstream population, simply because they are a part of the fabric of the structures of society. But these same situations can pose ethical problems when interpreted by and through Christian consciousness. Buttrick argues, "We are able, in some minimal manner, to discriminate understandings in Christ from understandings common to our in-the-world humanity."[12] As Christians, we interpret the world in which we live as humans, while at the same time, we interpret events as Christians. Buttrick further shares, "Christian consciousness is double—we know we are worldly in the world, but we also know we are being saved."[13] We are in the world, but not of this world (John 15:19). In Christ, we are new creatures (2 Cor 5:17), transformed by the renewing of our mind (Rom 12:2). Two situations come to mind.

Immigration has been a crisis since our country's inception. From the Chinese Exclusion Act of 1882, to the push to build a border wall, the nation has grappled with immigration. When does immigration fit into the structure of Christian consciousness? When does it become the business of Christians and the church? Is immigration only something that the state should concern itself with? Should we advocate for families with children born in the United States to have a swift, uncomplicated path to US citizenship? Whenever human lives are adversely affected, the church should be willing to care about and confront the social crises at hand.

Our nation is a nation of immigrants. Immigrants are our image-bearing neighbors. With more than 45 million people in our country making up the immigrant population, our lives are intertwined with those whom we refer to as immigrants. They are our coworkers, neighbors, employees, friends, spouses, children, students, church members, teammates, and business partners. Some see the growing immigrant population as a threat to job security, public safety, and even national and cultural predictability. For others, while these concerns are genuine, there is another side to the coin. Many immigrants are fleeing countries, seeking asylum in America and a better life for their families and children. Both instances are among the reasons that many of our forefathers came to this country.

[12.] Buttrick, 415.
[13.] Buttrick, 414.

As a citizen in the world, we are concerned about the threats mentioned above, but as citizens of the kingdom of God, we interpret such
concerns with eyes of love, justice, and mercy. As citizens, we want
job opportunities for our communities and in our communities. We
should also care about those caught in the web of poverty, while we
shed a "me first" concept of human flourishing. In the social crisis
sermon template, a contemporary crisis such as immigration should
point the preacher to focus on values that the Christian community
should share, such as the importance of human agency, the value of
family, God's vision for the orphan and widow, and mercy.

Another example of a concern of Christian consciousness is about
how to make communities safe and whole. In many urban communities, crime is a significant problem. No one can dispute this reality. Equally undeniable is the fact that the people who live in those
communities want to be safe, raise children without fear, and see
their property appreciate in value. One way to mitigate the scourge
of crime is to increase the presence of law enforcement. Most law
enforcement personnel and police agencies advocate for the best and
latest weaponry available. The 1033 Program has been the vehicle by
which many law enforcement agencies across the country are able to
outfit their departments with military-grade tactical gear and armored
vehicles.[14] Over 8,000 law enforcement agencies have benefited from
around $7.4 billion worth of property, donated from the surplus of
supplies from the Department of Defense by only paying the cost of
shipping.[15] From a law enforcement perspective, this is a win-win. The
Department of Defense provides the best of the best equipment, and
it helps strapped municipalities on law-enforcement budgets.

Yet for most residents of these communities, the militarization of
police departments is unacceptable. For them, their communities are
hyper-policed and underprotected. These citizens argue that their
communities need better, more innovative schools, more outreach
and spiritual support from churches, better mental health resources,

---

14. *Defense Logistics Agency: The Nation's Combat Logistics Support Agency*, "DLA Disposition
Services, Join the 1033 Program," https://www.dla.mil/DispositionServices/Offers/Reutilization
/LawEnforcement/JoinTheProgram.aspx/

15. Brain Barrett, "The Pentagon's Hand-Me-Downs Helped Militarize Police. Here's How," *WIRED*,
June 2, 2020, https://www.wired.com/story/pentagon-hand-me-downs-militarize-police-1033-program/.

and robust social programs. They contend that the millions of dollars spent on military-grade equipment could easily guarantee the implementation of these programs. As a citizen of both the crime-infested community and the kingdom of God, matters like the militarization of police agencies come onto center stage, because they involve life and humanity. Stopping crime does not necessarily mean a better quality of life for communities that need so much more than an end to crime.

Usually, the contemporary social crisis is complicated and divisive. Multiple personal convictions and differing opinions may exist about its origin and solution, or even its existence and reality. Some don't consider racism to be a systemic problem. Some communities would not register the drug abuse epidemic as a significant crisis. Others see these concerns as individual choices, not deserving of communal attention. These two social crises are among many that are deserving of Christian proclamation, because the people most affected are our neighbors. The social crisis sermon that aims to address public issues, of which the community should be aware because they have significance, is Christian proclamation that develops congregations to intentionally care about and confront the crises in their neighbor's community in the power of the Holy Spirit.

Concern for the Hearer

Chapter two focused on the sacred anthropologist and the preacher's responsibility to apply the five "R's" of sacred anthropology. These steps will assist the preacher in understanding or exegeting the hearer; a vital component of effective preaching. Social crisis preaching has always been a delicate task, requiring wisdom, grace, and sensitivity to the vast array of political, social, and cultural views in the pews. When preparing your sermon, there are three things to consider to help you measure a concern for the hearer: (1) internal questions preachers must ask themselves to measure their understanding of the congregation, (2) the method of approach (inductive, deductive, semi-inductive), and (3) pertinent questions raised to the congregation in the sermon.

First, concerns for the hearer begin with the questions preachers must ask themselves: How well do I know this congregation or the people hearing my sermon? What are the convictions, beliefs, and fears that this congregation shares about the crisis at hand? How might this congregation differ in their convictions and opinions about it? What are the demographics of the congregation?

These questions prevent preachers from taking anything for granted about the hearer, including the congregation's knowledge about the crisis. They also encourage sensitivity. Some crises take a psychological and emotional toll on those affected. Preachers must be aware of how the church is coping with the crisis during sermon preparation. Even if the Word of truth opposes the hearer's worldview, beliefs, and experiences, preachers are better positioned to persuade when they understand their hearer's experiences.

The social crisis preacher must decide what method and style of preaching will be most effective for the congregation. Concern for the hearer is measured by communicating the Bible's truths and how those truths influence the social crisis the sermon is called to address. Will the truth of the Bible be communicated in an inductive approach or deductive approach, or a combination of both?

My approach is informed by the text, the congregation (ethnicity, geography, age, political affiliation, degree of knowledge about the issue), and the social crisis and its urgency. An inductive approach may be suitable when preaching about a sensitive subject to an audience that may not be well informed about the crisis at hand, or who may be resistant to the biblical application the text calls for. If I am preaching to instill hope to communities battered by distressing economic and environmental issues, I will be more direct and deliberate in communicating the all-sustaining power of God, as evidenced in the text, by the power of the Holy Spirit.

Smith, Sr., in his "Lyman Beecher Lectures" in 1983, offered the "miniature inductive" approach as a suggestion in the introduction. Smith, Sr. believed that the miniature inductive method "softens the blow of the presentation of the major point," and that, "the introduction moves gently but positively on to the basic thesis of the sermon. It employs a brief indirect procedure to make a direct announcement of a position and call to action."[16] The sermon must not jump immediately to solutions. Doing so can communicate that the preacher has not considered the hearer's experience. Jesus, as the Word made

---

16. Smith, Sr., *Social Crisis Preaching*, 92–93 (see intro., n. 10).

flesh, met people where they were. Preachers must do the same as we escort the Word of God to encounter the people of God.

I am very intentional about posing penetrating questions to the congregation and using two to three seconds of sacred silence for them to ponder and wrestle with the ethical concerns and tensions introduced by the text. In the sermon at the end of the chapter, I ask, "Have you ever been of the mind-set that 'more is better'?" I then asked, "What does the mind-set of more do to those who are perpetually dealing with less?" This allows hearers to weigh their conviction and opinion against the truth of Scripture or an alternate point posed by the preacher. Long says, "The task of preaching is not to set out some reality in life and then to go to the Bible to find extra wisdom. It is instead to tell the story of the Bible so clearly that it calls into question and ultimately redefines what we think we know of reality and what we call wisdom in the first place."[17] Posing penetrating, challenging questions does this.

Samuel Proctor's relevant question is critical in this discussion. He borrowed the dialectical approach for the search for truth from Georg Wilhelm Hegel (1770–1831) and adapted it for the African American pulpit. Proctor added homiletical functionality to *thesis, antithesis,* and *synthesis* and then included "the relevant question." According to Proctor, "in order to give the sermon vitality, currency, application, and relevance, the next step is to ask a 'so what?' question, the relevant question—the most relevant question that anyone would normally raise after hearing the antithesis and thesis."[18] This method introduces tension to the congregation and confronts them with life's most urgent moral and ethical questions. The "relevant questions" call congregations to self-analysis and examination, to confession and repentance, and to forgiveness and restoration.

Theological Relevance

Without theological relevance, the act of proclamation cannot be legitimately called a Christian sermon—it would be more akin to a civic speech. Helmut Thielicke's sermons sought to bring theological

---

[17.] Thomas Long, *The Witness of Preaching* (Louisville: Westminster, 1989), 35
[18.] Samuel D. Proctor, *The Certain Sound of the Trumpet: Crafting a Sermon of Authority* (Valley Forge, PA: Judson, 1994), 28.

relevance to social concerns. When he preached about a biblical theme or a doctrinal subject, he tied it to the *"Sitz im Leben"* (life situation). Marvin Dirks testifies of Thielicke's belief that "if preaching is to be relevant it must be based on a Christian anthropology in which the preacher sees man in the world and not a part of the world."[19] I might add, the preacher must see God's purpose for man in the world. Theological relevance is a wedding of anthropology to Christian theology, officiated by the sermon from the Christian Scriptures.

In my sermon "The Myth of More," the theological relevance is stewardship. The theological relevance of this sermon also points to the idolatry of money and identifies human greed as the root cause of our failure to care for the poor, widow, foreigners, and orphans (Exod 22:21–24; Deut 27:19; Zech 7:9–10; Jas 2:1–7). The crisis is a growing concern, exasperated by a pandemic where people are anxious, afraid, and responding with individualistic motives instead of trusting God and having concern for their neighbor. This sermon is about more than dollars and cents. It calls the church away from the ambitious, competitive spirit of the world and back into a life where we "seek first the kingdom of God and his righteousness" (Matt 6:33a).

One of the most egregious atrocities that has ever faced the African American community in the United States, and as a result, denied thousands of Black Americans the opportunity to pass on wealth to their posterity, was the injustice of redlining.[20] In his multiple award-winning essays about redlining and housing discrimination, Coates explains, "From the 1930s through the 1960s, black people across the country were largely cut out of the legitimate home-mortgage market through means both legal and extralegal."[21] White communities tried incessantly to keep Black families out of their all-white communities for fear that their property value would decrease whenever a Black family moved in. In the early 1960s, redlining and housing discrimination became an ethical issue that white pastors were forced to weigh in on. Addressing the issue, Thielicke insists that this issue bore theological

---

[19.] Marvin Dirks, *Laymen Look at Preaching: Lay Expectation Factors in Relation to the Preaching of Helmut Thielicke* (North Quincy, MA: Christopher, 1972), 167.

[20.] For one of the most insightful studies on redlining, see Richard Rothstein, *The Color of Law: A Forgotten History of How Our Government Segregated America* (New York: Liveright, 2017).

[21.] Coates, "The Case for Reparations," (intro, n. 8).

relevance and was no mere social or civic issue to which the church could turn a blind eye.

In his second trip to the United States, a six-month lecture tour, Thielicke was invited to speak at universities and churches across the country. The topic of these lectures ranged from the inspiration of the Bible, the virgin birth, speaking in tongues, the Nazi regime, racial integration, and numerous other topics. A year later, Thielicke recorded those lectures in his book *Between Heaven and Earth*. He brought the Word of God and theology to bear on housing discrimination and racial integration in all-white neighborhoods. By the time Thielicke had given his insight about the problem, it had come to the front step of many American churches, knocking on the door of the pastor's study, demanding to be answered. Thielicke noted

> The really decisive question arises where one has to make up one's mind whether Negro people should be allowed to settle in a white neighborhood. You certainly know that property values fall abruptly as soon as the first Negro residents appear on a street or district of the city. Hence anybody who sells his house to a Negro buyer incurs the hatred of his former neighbors. There is, as it were, a kind of community conspiracy among the house owners. What should our attitude be on this? This is precisely where we ministers are repeatedly confronted with the hardest question of conscience.[22]

These are the matters with which social crisis preaching involves itself and to which sacred anthropologists are called to provide guidance. Thielicke's answer called for the church not to avoid these matters or pretend they did not exist. He continues

> Consequently, the real truth of the situation could be that it is not because the Negroes are moving in that the whites are afraid and move out, but rather that the Negroes move in because the whites are afraid. I cannot help it, but here again I believe that

---

[22.] Helmut Thielicke, *Between Heaven and Earth: Conversation with American Christians* (Cambridge, UK: Lutterworth, 1964), chap. 7, Kindle.

these are not primarily economic and social processes, but simply neuroses. And this is exactly the reason why I believe that here the church has a special obligation. For if this is true, then all this falls within the competence of the church's pastoral care, not only as it admonishes people to practice neighborly love, but also as it summons them to be sober and realistic and passes on our Lord's words "Be not afraid" in every conceivable variation. Perhaps then it will be given to the church here and there to put a stop to that "law" of economic depreciation—and show it up as being not a law at all but only the economic after effect of a fever.[23]

Cleverly and insightfully, Thielicke asserted that this was not only a race problem but a class prejudice akin to a neurosis rooted in the sin of self-idolatry or a kind of group or race narcissism. Thielicke adds

In the same way one must very soberly examine whether this aversion to a Negro neighbor is really based only on racial defensive instincts or whether it may not have social and cultural causes. We know that on the average the Negro people, through no fault of their own, do not have anywhere near the same living and cultural standards as the white population. We also know that often those who have rapidly become well-to-do and are able to afford a more expensive house in a good residential area are not always the most likable exemplars of their race—whether white or Negro. Might not the whites be succumbing to a self-delusion if they think they are resisting the moving in of a Negro only for racial reasons when in reality they are averse to having somebody near them who is on a lower social or cultural level?[24]

The preacher's theological orientation must wed theology with a keen awareness of the depth and breadth of social concerns. But in some instances, preachers may not be convinced that the sermon should be concerned with the death-dealing issues that haunt the local church members. The theological function is critical to the social crisis preacher

23. Thielicke, chap. 7, Kindle.
24. Thielicke, chap. 7, Kindle.

in part because the preacher's theological orientation is also foundational to social crisis preaching and ministry in general. If the preacher
believes that the Bible and theology should not be concerned with
social and political issues, then social crisis preaching does not exist.

Interdisciplinary Content

The interdisciplinary content that goes into the social crisis sermon is the
work of the sacred anthropologist. The sacred anthropologist serves as a
resource for and about their neighbor's community. Disciplines outside
of theology are the tools that sacred anthropologists often use to mine the
truth about humanity from mountains of misconceptions. Social crisis
preaching should include disciplines outside of theology (economics,
civics, sociology, anthropology, culture) in the sermon. People live in a
world where they and those they love make up the data and statistics that
tell the story of their lives. In the Bible, there are potent details disclosed
in statistics and data. Examples include the twelve tribes of Israel (Gen
48:17–49:27; Josh 4:2), Gideon's army being reduced from 22,000 to
300 (Judg 7), John seeing a number that no man could number (Rev
7:1–9), the size of the former temple compared to the size of the second temple (Ezra 3:8–13), five loaves and two fish (Matt 14:13–21),
Jesus rising on the third day (Luke 24:1–7), etc. One could argue that
Christian theology comprises data, statistics, geography, anthropology,
and mythology drenched in the divine. Thus, all truth is God's truth.

I often use statistics in my social crisis sermons. Although statistics
can be manipulated, some are objective, unbiased, and reliable. Most
facts of history are hard to dispute. Some statistics and data can be
collected from politically neutral sources and agencies. For example,
a responsible social crisis preacher confronting the crisis of abortion
would be wise to use the statistics showing the number of abortions
and the reasons women give for having abortions.

Honest and responsible preaching about abortion must consider
other vital data, such as statistics about the root social causes of abortion, including lack of access to healthcare, poverty, and dysfunctional
family units resulting from poverty. Other factors include the hopelessness that some "would-be" parents feel when they consider bringing a child into a world of food deserts, low-performing schools, no

recreational parks, or into crime ridden communities where sports and education programs are nonexistent. Some parents only see a world that is not kid-friendly and unfortunately their decision to terminate a pregnancy is rooted in these and other social traumas. While there should never be a compromise on biblical values, when we "only" focus on spiritual reasons, to persuade people who daily face social and economic hardships, preaching can be perceived as legalistic and moralistic. In the feeding of the five thousand, Jesus demonstrated the wisdom preachers should possess, when he compassionately considered the physical and economic needs of the masses (Matt 14:13–21). Jesus fed the hungry crowd before delivering transforming spiritual truths. Preachers must consider the fact that hungry, poor people need bread to stay alive, as well as the bread of life.

One approach to addressing abortion only relates and relays statistics about the increasing number of abortions annually. This approach will lead some people to conclude that the only solution to eliminate abortion is to make abortion illegal by voting for political candidates that would ban abortions. This approach reduces abortion to an abstract, ethereal idea void of personal impact, ignoring the ever-present realities that lead individuals to conclude that abortion is their only viable option.

Social crisis preaching is concerned about people and communities. The preacher is responsible for helping the congregation understand how social crises affect people. The sermon prompts the congregation to consider a variety of questions: What is the relationship between poverty and those who are considering abortion? What healthcare and prenatal services are available to those considering abortion? What is the quality of education in the communities of those who represent abortion statistics? Such questions humanize the conversation, leading people to be concerned with the reasons why people are led to abortion clinics. Perhaps addressing these underlying motivations will in effect decrease abortion rates. This consideration will only happen when preachers gather comprehensive statistics and data that consider the whole person and the communities in which they live.

Division in communities often arises because of misperception and misunderstanding about the people most affected by the crises at the heart of the division. When people draw conclusions, other people, usually their neighbors, are hurt.

In a sermon preached from Matthew 25, Proctor demonstrates how valuable interdisciplinary content can be in sermon effectiveness. In this sermon, Proctor disdains the church's bent toward militarism by decrying our "obsession with bombs and tanks and first-strike capability."[25] Proctor states

> The social prophet, the one who every Sunday looks at the failures of the institutions of society and the unraveling of the social fabric . . . . along with this social and prophetic word, the people need education in religious matters and comfort in life's crisis moments; they need to be given an impetus to serve, to participate, and to create alliances to address the issues that are so glaring in the pastor's sermons. So the social prophet must remember the total menu and the need for a complete diet in the weekly sermons.[26]

Proctor could articulate political and social ideologies and examine them under the light of the gospel.

Smith Jr. informs how Thielicke intentionally offered "interdisciplinary courses on the cultural life, anthropology, theology, and history and made it a requirement for a theology student."[27] I am of total resolve that seminarians should be encouraged to read widely and be equipped to apologetically defend the faith from the assaults of secular theorists and religious fundamentalists who either misuse or exclude social sciences. Social sciences and interdisciplinary subjects, examined under the light of the truth of the Word of God, have the potential to help the preacher better understand the complexities of the systemic and institutional barriers that prevent human flourishing.

Theologically Comprehensible Language

In order to have a theological function, theological subjects and language must be used. In concern for the hearer, the preacher will add color, style, and flavor for a crystal-clear image of theological subjects

---

[25.] Samuel Proctor, "Proctor1983 3337," YouTube, LTSP Communications, https://www.youtube.com/watch?v=Gjxi8RIY9GY.

[26.] Proctor, *The Certain Sound of the Trumpet*, 5.

[27.] Robert Smith, Jr., 32.

and language. When the theological language is comprehensible, hearers will not only be theologically informed, but they will better understand the God and the faith that has laid claim to their lives. If the preacher cannot "make it plain," the listener will be bored and struggle to understand how the Bible, through the social crisis sermon, has something to say to their lives.

In the African American worship service, one can hear a seasoned deacon or church mother on any given Sunday morning, during the rhythmic call and response of the preaching moment, cry out, "Make it plain!" Social crisis preaching at its most potent is spoken in plain language. Social crisis preaching cannot afford to be separated from the tenets of the Christian faith: salvation, sanctification, trinitarian theology, the deity of Christ, for example; however, throughout church history, scholars, church fathers, and theologians have often used the academy's language to communicate the tenets of the faith. Words such as *homoiousios* (similar substance), *homoousios* (same substance), transubstantiation, consubstantiation, and dispensationalism have had a place in the church for centuries, but they do little to edify the church unless the preacher can provide their definition in a manner that a child might understand.

Concerning this reality, Dietrich Bonhoeffer's words ring true, "The time when people could be told everything by means of words, whether theological or pious, is over."[28] Unfortunately, we live in a time when many in our pews don't know the biblical story, let alone the biblical story told in rich theological language. When preachers use comprehensible theological language, the Word of God goes out and does not return void; rather it accomplishes the purpose for which it was sent (Isa 55:11).

Social crisis preachers are most effective when they can communicate the social relevance of the gospel and the intricate details of the actual social crises to congregants of various socioeconomic communities. For instance, using Thielicke as an example, Dirks concludes, "Having listened to Thielicke lecture to students at the University of Hamburg, the writer is aware that there is a considerable difference

---

[28.] Dietrich Bonhoeffer, *Letters and Papers from Prison*, trans. Reginald Fuller, Frank Clark, et al., ed. Eberhard Bethge (New York: Simon & Schuster, 1997), 279.

both in vocabulary and in content of the lectures as compared to the sermons intended for the general listening audience at Michaelis."[29] Dirks makes the point that Thielicke often took pains to explain theological words and doctrinal subjects and their "existential relevance of the doctrines and dogmas of the church."[30] The sacred anthropologist is willing to feel the hurts and pain of the person and community in crisis and then formulate language from the places of deep hurt and heartbreak.

Like any other mode of preaching, social crisis preaching requires the preacher to contextualize language, use vivid imagination, metaphors, and explanation to simplify the sometimes "hard to comprehend" theological language of the church and academy. Smith, Jr.'s book, *Doctrine That Dances*, provides an invaluable treatment on this matter. Smith, Jr. promotes "a metaphorical rationale for doctrinal preaching" by advising that the presentation of doctrine and biblical characters in the sermon is best conveyed through the use of metaphor.[31] He writes, "To preach only to the heads of people puts one in the category of a 'big-headed preacher.' A preacher who excludes the heads of the congregation and totally focuses on the congregation's heart is a 'beheaded preacher.' Preaching must have a bifocal trajectory: it must focus on both head and heart."[32] Jesus spoke in simple terms and used parables and metaphors, allowing his audience to relate easily to his teachings. Whether it was an eschatological lesson (Matt 25) or an ethical one (Luke 16:1–13), people were transformed, and his word resonated, "because he was teaching them like one who had authority, and not like their scribes" (Matt 7:29).

Courage to Confront

Massey contends, "Radicality in the sermon engages the hearer. It makes him know that he is being confronted, that necessity is being

---

[29] Dirks, *Laymen Look at Preaching*, 165–66.

[30] Dirks, 168.

[31] A metaphor is a part of speech. Smith defines metaphor as "an extension of meaning through the comparison of one thing to another." For argument and uses of metaphor in the Bible, see Smith, Jr., *Doctrine That Dances*, 30 (intro, n. 30)

[32] Smith, Jr., 111.

laid upon him to respond. True preaching is always confrontational."[33] Social crisis preaching is not an eloquent diatribe that simply identifies problems and introduces solutions; rather, it demands that the hearer break from any and all political, racial, economic, or theological loyalties that are complicit in social crises.[34] To move congregations beyond mere abstract thinking and social media fights about social crises, pastors must possess Holy Spirit-inspired courage to confront the congregation's social issues. Social crisis preaching challenges religious and civil corruption through the Word of God in the power of the Spirit.

In one of Proctor's most popular and widely acclaimed sermons "The Scratch Line," he brilliantly calls every listener to remember the undeserved benefits we inherit, and to use them to serve and help those who have inherited undeserved misfortune.[35] The scratch line is that hypothetical position into which we are all born, having earned nothing, achieved nothing, and being indebted to everyone. Proctor eloquently, and in picturesque language, describes those born below the scratch line and those born above the scratch line. He describes this further in his book *Samuel Proctor: My Moral Odyssey*, where he writes,

> a further premise of this genuine community is that those of us who have inherited opportunities and sponsorship that we never deserved or earned are morally bound to enable those who inherited disadvantages and obstacles that they did not deserve or earn to achieve the same outcomes that we are enabled to achieve, with our unearned and undeserved opportunities and scholarship.[36]

A major challenge of social crisis preaching is challenging those above "the scratch line" to recognize their dependency on God and the other people who make their positions and wealth possible and to use their resources and position for social uplift.

At the time of this writing, the news is still swirling about Jeff Bezos,

---

[33.] Massey, *The Responsible Pulpit* (see intro, n. 26)

[34.] Tyshawn Gardner, "An Analysis of Prophetic Radicalism in the Social Crisis Preaching of Kelly Miller Smith, Sr.," (PhD diss., Southern Baptist Theological Seminary, 2019), 164.

[35.] Samuel Dewitt Proctor, "The Scratch Line, Rev. Dr. Samuel Dewitt Proctor-SDPC," YouTube video, *YouTube*, posted January 21, 2011, https://www.youtube.com/watch?v=X1la3TAxu8w.

[36.] Samuel Proctor, *Samuel Proctor: My Moral Odyssey* (Valley Forge PA: Judson, 1989), 150.

the founder and executive chairman of Amazon, the richest man on Earth, and Richard Branson, billionaire founder of the Virgin Group, a venture capital firm. Both men took private trips to the outer limits of Earth's gravity. They flew into space in July 2021, each aboard their own private spacecraft—Bezos in the New Shepard and Branson in the VSS Unity. Bids for a seat on the Bezos' space flight closed at $28 million. Reports are that Bezos' trip to space cost an estimated $2.54 million per minute. The trip lasted a total of eleven minutes.[37] Spokespersons for Blue Origin, the private aerospace manufacturer and spaceflight service company that built New Shepard, inform that two additional flights are scheduled for this year alone.[38]

Proctor's sermon speaks to a world amused with "for-fun" space travel but unmoved by struggling families, many of whom are employees of the billionaires that flew into space in July 2021. Those born above the scratch line have an obligation to help those born below the scratch line.

Neither the church nor the social crisis preacher should be passive, unmoved, unbothered, and quiet where there are social injustices. Courage in the social crisis preaching moment does not mean that we excite a flesh-inspired, rough, insensitive boldness, but that we exercise firm, grace-filled speech (Gal 5:6) that emanates from a compassionate, loving heart. Social crisis preaching will call us to ask and answer: To whom does my allegiance lie? I have found that when preachers confront sensitive issues, even if people disagree, they return another Sunday to listen to another sermon, because they sense sincerity, honesty, and respect, even in messages that confront their long-held beliefs.

Redemptive Takeaway

The social crisis sermon may begin with acknowledging a painful situation; however, it should end by offering the hope that lies in Christ. Always. The redemptive takeaway is the component in the social crisis sermon template that will require the preacher to find the light in the

---

[37.] Marina Koren, "Jeff Bezos Knows Who Paid for Him to Go to Space," *Atlantic*, July 20, 2021, https://www.theatlantic.com/science/archive/2021/07/jeff-bezos-blue-origin-successful-flight/619484/.

[38.] Kenneth Chang, "What will it cost to fly on New Shepard?," *New York Times*, July 20, 2021, https://www.nytimes.com/2021/07/20/science/cost-to-fly-blue-origin-bezos.html.

darkness of the social crisis. Here are the questions preachers must wrestle with at this point in sermon preparation: What is the hope of Christ concerning this social crisis? How does the Word of God speak to this crisis by offering hope"

The redemptive takeaway—like the biblical background information, the contemporary social crisis, the theological relevance, interdisciplinary content, and the theologically comprehensible language, can be built in with each move or point throughout the sermon.

THE MYTH OF MORE, LUKE 12:13–34

The excerpt below is part of the introduction of my sermon "The Myth of More" from Luke 12:13–34. Here, the social crisis sermon template is brought to light. I will use the sermon to provide a step-by-step analysis on how to design a social crisis sermon.

SERMON EXCERPT

This virus that we are facing has exposed the greed, narcissism, and corruption from multibillion-dollar CEOs all the way down to the minimum-wage consumer who goes into a store to horde everything on the shelf. This sermon has shed light on our propensity to idolize money and material things, thus becoming unfaithful stewards. It has also exposed the charlatans in the church, by pulling the covers off the lightweight theology that has packed churches by selling the poison of prosperity-laced messages that exploit those who are wishing, waiting, and wanting their "season to arrive," their "ship to come in," and their "year of increase," where they "will never be broke another day in their life." Yes, the myth of more has created myopic mindsets! In verse 17, the rich man "thought to himself." Myopic means to lack foresight, unable to see far off. When you are nearsighted, you can't read distant signs. This man could see no further than himself! He had a myopic mindset. People who have myopic mindsets are first, limited in love, second, limited in language, and third, limited in (out) look.

Outline of Components in the SCS Template

I. **Myopic Mindset**: In verse 17 "he thought to himself." Near-sighted people can only see in the distance—limited insight. Myopic minds are also limited:

    A. **Limited in Love**: Generosity is an expression of love. Greed/covetousness is a form of self-love. Self-love is limited love. Verse 34 says, "For where your treasure is, there will your heart be also" (ESV). Self-love vs. neighbor-love (Mark 12:31).

        1. Interdisciplinary Content: Data of median incomes, minimum wage, poverty vs. CEO earnings.

        2. Theological Relevance/Comprehensible Language: coveting explained through an illustration of "supersize." Greed hurts the poor. Wealth doesn't automatically trickle down, as we see in verse 19. Greed is not a reflection of the imago Dei.

        3. Redemptive Takeaway: Christ's love is unlimited because it is not based on what we have but who we are. So we should view our neighbor and treat them with Christ's love.

    B. **Limited in Language**: He was exclusive in language. He uses "I" or "my" over ten times. The language of myopic minds is the personal pronoun "my"—my world, my kind, my school district, my race, my country, etc.

        1. Interdisciplinary Content: The Declaration of Independence, three-fifths compromise in the US Constitution, Frederick Douglass's speech, "What, to the American Slave, is Your Fourth of July?"

        2. Theologically Comprehensible Language: agape/hesed defined and illustrated.

        3. Redemptive Takeaway: God uses the language of "all."

    C. **Limited in (Out) Look**: Verse 15b says, "For one's life does not consist in the abundance of his possessions." What are the principles that govern how you view the poor? Does your vote reflect an outlook for the poor, and that you are looking out for the poor? Do you have a biblical outlook on possessions? Secular outlook? Self-preservation outlook? Privilege and superiority outlook? Look out and look for the kingdom. Verse 31: Are you seeking the kingdom? How do we seek the kingdom? Seek what matters to our heavenly Father. The poor matter!

1. Interdisciplinary Content: In this sermon I use statistics from Alabama Appleseed (https://www.alabamaapple-seed.org/broke-report/) about predatory lending and payday loan institutions and their devastating effects on the poor.

2. Theological Comprehensible Language: I explain the word eschatology, since the question raised in verse 31 is about the kingdom.

3. Redemptive Takeaway: Believers need a biblical outlook on material possessions; one that is rooted in God's stewardship design and plan. This outlook takes the plight of the unsaved and the poor into account. God is looking out for the poor (verse 28). One day he will be arbitrator and judge, judging the greedy and delivering the poor and oppressed. A biblical outlook, reveals to us that God is looking out for the poor.

In the "Myth of More" sermon, the redemptive takeaway also takes an eschatological tone, proclaimed in the last subpoint. It takes its clue from verses 31, 33, and 34. The sermon addresses greed and its manifesting forms of economic exploitation and lack of neighborly concern. But it also provides the cure for greed, the Father's care for his children! As shown in the outline, the preaching text offers a segue for celebrating how God provides for the poor and those in need (vv. 26–32). The sermon will conclude with a call to action to generosity and advocacy (vv. 33–34). In this way, the redemptive takeaways are also in the celebration at the conclusion.

Fulfillment of the Social Crisis Sermon

The final component of the social crisis sermon template is direct and to the point. After the manuscript has been written and the sermon preached, the question that must be asked is: Does the sermon work to develop the congregation to care about and confront the social crisis in their neighbor's community in the power of the Holy Spirit? This component can be measured in the application of the sermon. A note of wisdom is appropriate here. The application that the social crisis sermon calls for should require the congregation to seek the power, wisdom, and grace of the Holy Spirit. Sometimes calling for a different "outlook," as one of the sermon's applications below does, requires the Holy Spirit to transform made-up minds and cold hearts. Sermon applications that fail to call for sacrifice and dependency on the Holy Spirit can lean toward humanism and moralism. In the "Myth of More," I call for a new "outlook" on materialism and oppressive economic systems, and for the congregation to "look out" for the poor in a manner that shows God's concern and favor for them.

A SOCIAL CRISIS SERMON

Text

Luke 12:13–34. Within this text is the Lukan parable, often labeled "The Parable of the Rich Fool." But it must be interpreted within the larger framework of Jesus's teaching in this section of Luke. I believe this sermon must extend beyond its traditional division that stops at verse 21. Also, notice verse 22 that provides a hint as to why Jesus taught this particular parable to his disciples. It was not only to address the disagreement between brothers in verses 13–15. These two bookends, greed and anxiety, are the focus of this parable, and they speak to the crisis I will address: the relationship of anxiety and greed in the COVID-19 pandemic.

Title

The sermon title, "The Myth of More," captures the idea of the pericope and the theology of the preaching passage found in verse 15b: "Watch out and be on guard against all greed, because one's life is not in the abundance of his possessions." I chose the word "myth" to express the erroneous thinking of the "rich man" in the text. The title allowed for acrostics that I felt would be short and easy for the audience to remember.

Genre
Gospel/parable. This genre allowed me to approach this text in its natural form by being didactic through the principles of the parables. The genre also provided an opportunity to contemporize the rich man in a narrative-like method.

Social Crisis Sermon Statement
"Wherever greed exists it is a sign that we have a self-centered outlook that hinders us from looking out for others."

Biblical Background/ Social Crisis in the Text
In the gospel of Luke, Jesus teaches the disciples valuable theological lessons through parables. In this passage, Jesus is teaching his disciples, who are of meager means, about covetousness, that can consume low-income as well as wealthy people.

Contemporary Social Crisis
The COVID-19 pandemic exposed greed on multiple levels, from multimillion-dollar corporations to low-income individuals scamming for Paycheck Protection Program[39] loans, to the hoarding of household necessities from the shelves of convenience and supermarket stores. Greed is infectious, and when the rich consume all the resources, the poor suffer even to the point of death.

Concerns for Hearer
Semi-inductive preaching method. Demographic considerations relative to the sermon: 10–15 percent professionals, 40 percent blue-collar, 35 percent middle class, 10 percent lower socioeconomic hourly workers, 5 percent teenage workers and working college students, most

---

[39.] During the height of the COVID-19 pandemic, the U.S. Department of Treasury implemented the CARES Act, whereby through the Paycheck Protection Program, small businesses were provided resources to cover payroll or to hire back employees who may have been laid off due to state and government mandating the temporary shutdown of businesses and government entities to prevent the spread of COVID-19. The first CARES package was $659 billion. See https://home.treasury.gov/policy-issues/coronavirus/assistance-for-small-businesses/paycheck-protection-program.

with student loans. I preached this message at Plum Grove Baptist Church, where I served as pastor for nineteen years. I have engaged the pre-proclamation function of the preacher with this congregation as their pastor.

Theological Relevance
The theological relevance of this sermon is stewardship. This sermon also speaks to the relevance of modern day idolatry and greed, which are also sins that are addressed in the Word of God.

Interdisciplinary Content
Current minimum wage rate, wealth rates among racial demographics, number of millionaires, billionaires in America, median family income, student debt, disposable income of Black families.

Theologically Comprehensible Language
In the sermon, coveting (verse 15) is defined and explained in the illustration of "supersize." Fast food restaurant employees offer "more" and "bigger" for a little cost through a "supersized" meal. But whenever we pay more for supersized meals, two things happen: (1) we end up wasting it because we don't or can't eat it all, or (2) we do consume it all, but later we find that we are still hungry. Coveting is wanting and obtaining more (supersize) of what you don't need and can't use, simply because you want it and can obtain it. Coveting never pays because in the end it is never fulfilling.

Courage
This sermon forced me to confront my own convictions and ambitions about having and obtaining more. Many of the members in my congregation were either guilty of hoarding or felt the frustration of not finding household and personal necessities due to the hoarding of others, as a response to the fear of COVID-19. In this sermon, courage was displayed in confronting fear and condemning the actions (in this case greed) that Christians sometimes justify just because they are afraid. Courage also challenges the congregation to a life of simplicity and sharing amidst a world where the ambition to have "more" is considered admirable.

Redemptive Takeaway
The myth of having more material possessions without a willingness to share more is a sign that we lack more of the mind of Christ. Christ is our sufficiency. God is just, and he will care for those who trust him. The remedy to the sin of greed and anxiety is trusting the all-sufficient God and being faithful to extend our help to the poor.

Fulfillment of SCS
Yes. If the congregation follows the application the sermon calls for, the results would be a greater call to serve, increased giving in stewardship, reconsideration of personal goals, and a willingness to share.

CONCLUSION

The social crisis sermon template can be used to help preachers deliver powerful and relevant sermons that can best be described as "biblically-rooted, Spirit-enabled proclamation that develops and drives congregations to compassionately care for and radically confront social crises in the communities where their neighbors live, work, worship, and play." The aim of this template is to help preachers develop a deeper awareness of the social matters around them, and to engage in a genuine and redemptive imagination of how communities beset in crises ought to function in light of the transforming power of the cross of Christ and his resurrection.

CHAPTER 4:

SOCIAL CRISIS PREACHING DELIVERY CONSIDERATIONS

Today, preachers have countless resources at their disposal concerning sermon delivery methods.[1] Such practices generally focus on the use of eye contact, preaching with or without notes, body language, dress and attire, tone of voice, and lately, the use of technology and multimedia. Social crisis preaching delivery considerations will enable preachers to give captivating sermons, that not only grip and sustain the congregation's attention, but also aid in their spiritual formation. The delivery methods contained in this chapter will ensure that preachers develop a spirituality to sustain them in the demanding work of caring about and confronting social crises where their neighbors live, work and play. In this chapter we will focus on two major areas: (1) timing and balance and (2) rhetorical matters and concerns.

BALANCE AND TIMING

We should recall, a social crisis or social issue is public, that people know about it (or should know about it), and it affects people as a community. One may wonder when the "proper time" is to address a social crisis from the pulpit through a sermon? The short answer

---

[1.] For some of the most helpful advice on sermon delivery, see Jared Alcántara, "Preach Creatively," in *The Practices of Christian Preaching: Essentials for Effective Proclamation* (Grand Rapids: Baker, 2019), 155–84; Henry Mitchell, "Personal Style in Black Preaching," in *Black Preaching: The Recovery of a Powerful Art* (Nashville: Abingdon, 1990), 88–99; Hershael W. York and Bert Decker, "The Behavior Skills," in *Preaching with Bold Assurance: A Solid and Enduring Approach to Engaging Exposition* (Nashville: B&H, 2003), 221–60.

to this question is: always! As social beings living in a social world, humanity is, in a theological sense, in a constant state of crisis. We are fallen creatures who inhabit a fallen world. That means things are not as God intended: "for our struggle is not against flesh and blood, but against the rulers, against the authorities, against the cosmic powers of this darkness, against evil spiritual forces in the heavens" (Eph 6:12). Humans—Christian or not—are damaged by the effects of sin in this age. Thus, preaching should address some sort of communal, national, or global problem every Sunday morning.

The spiritual and the social are so intertwined that it is difficult to define some messages as strictly social crisis sermons. For instance, suicide is indeed a crisis in our contemporary world. It is a social issue because many of the causes of suicide lie outside of what we would deem spiritual matters. There are physiological and biological causes of suicide, chemical imbalances and mental disorders that are hereditary in nature. In addition, many are linked to the lack of access to mental healthcare and insurance, poverty, historic trauma, closure of mental health facilities, and a myriad of other causes that affect not only individuals but communities. In *World Psychiatry*, the official journal of the World Psychiatric Association, Maria A. Oquendo and Enrique Baca-Garcia write concerning suicide risk and behavior: "the presence of a psychiatric condition is certainly the most recognized risk factor for suicidal behavior. However, environmental risk factors such as unemployment, marital disruptions and financial crises are also clearly linked to risk."[2]

One cannot address suicide adequately and responsibly without emphasis on the spiritual condition. Some spiritual concerns related to suicide include the aid and comfort of the Holy Spirit in addressing the spiritual condition of the person, by emphasizing the spiritual gifts in the body of Christ to minister, counsel, and protect those who are contemplating suicide. So more accurate questions may be: When does a pastor preach sermons that are solely devoted to the major social crises that continuously affect their congregation? How often does a pastor preach about a major social crisis that affects the church members' neighbors?

These issues may include the constant state of poverty, crime, the

---

[2] Maria A. Oquendo and Enrique Baca-Garcia, "Suicidal Behavior Disorder as a Diagnostic Entity in the DSM-5 Classification System: Advantages Outweigh Limitations," *World Psychiatry*, June 2, 2014, accessed February 4, 2022, https://onlinelibrary.wiley.com/doi/10.1002/wps.20116.

state of the local education system, the pandemic, political corruption, sex and human trafficking, drug abuse, sexism, racism, child abuse, secularism, discrimination, economic exploitation of workers, and poor infrastructure in minority and poor communities, to name a few. Unless Scripture weighs in on the subject, the mere mention of such issues in the sermon does not automatically make it a social crisis sermon. In order to qualify as a social crisis sermon, it must also apply the principles and proposed practices dictated by the biblical text to a clearly identified current social crisis that adversely affects the congregation or the congregation's neighbors.

How often should the Word of God be brought to bear solely on a legitimate social crisis? Preachers who continuously address the sin of racism or discrimination as the central issue in the sermon could easily be perceived of as angry, bitter, vengeful, or lazy. More importantly, any preacher who practices this could not possibly be preaching the whole counsel of God, giving the congregation a steady, balanced diet that will "equip the saints for the work of ministry, to build up the body of Christ" (Eph 4:12).

Factors to Consider

On the other hand, the answer to the question, "How often does the preacher engage the text to address major social crises?" can be determined from the depth of the social involvement of the congregation. Has the congregation been involved in civic engagement (i.e., food drives, voter registration, hosting political forums, social causes, partnerships with social agencies, financial contribution to social agencies and causes)? Other determining factors could include how close the crisis is to the congregation, their loved ones, and the community where the church exists. How is the crisis affecting the congregation emotionally, mentally, and financially? How is it affecting their family structure? Is the congregation constantly dealing with or confronted with a social crisis daily, weekly, or monthly? Is it a recurring issue?

Additionally, one must consider other congregational needs as well. When does the preaching schedule allow for sermons that focus on marriage, raising children, matters of eschatology, the practice of spiritual disciplines or worship? To be sure, even such subjects that may not appear to be a "social issue" at face value, usually has a social application. In this case, a sermon focused on one of the subjects mentioned above may have a social implication in one of the homiletical points. Still, the sermon may not answer the question, "What does eschatology or raising children have to do with the social crisis we are currently facing?"

In addition, other factors to consider concerning the frequency of the social crisis sermon will include overlapping crisis concerns. For example, COVID-19 is a crisis in America, but the pandemic has exposed glaring health disparities in minority communities and among older citizens. Are there intersecting issues? Does the poverty crisis in a community contribute to the crime rates, substandard schools, inadequate health facilities, and mortality rates in that community? The most significant factor to consider is how social crisis preaching aids the spiritual formation and development of the church. Nurturing our spiritual health, developing our spiritual gifts, and serving in the power of the Spirit are essential to who we are as Christians. They are what distinguish us as the set-apart community, "a holy priesthood to offer spiritual sacrifices acceptable to God through Jesus Christ" (1 Pet 2:5b). For instance, Richard Foster, in his classic text, *Celebration of Discipline*, views service as a spiritual discipline. With the amount of sacrifice, self-denial, and humility involved, one can see how and why service would be included. Foster comments,

> Radical self-denial gives the feel of adventure. If we forsake all, we even have the chance of glorious martyrdom. But in service we must experience the many little deaths of going beyond ourselves. Service banishes us to the mundane, the ordinary, the trivial. In the Discipline of service there is also great liberty. Service enables us to say "no!" to the world's games of promotion and authority. It abolishes our need (and desire) for a "pecking order."[3]

Social crisis preaching can develop the discipleship program and also be a tool that the Holy Spirit uses to deepen the faith and enrich the spiritual lives of the congregation.

Whenever there is a national, global, or even community-wide crisis,

---

[3.] Richard Foster, *Celebration of Discipline: The Path to Spiritual Growth*, Special Anniversary Edition (New York: HarperCollins, 2018), 126–27, Kindle.

the timing of addressing the crisis is a major concern. Too long of a delay, or altogether avoiding the topic, will cause members to view the pastor as insensitive. In the summer of 2020, the nation and many churches sought to navigate the ever-present, controversial subject of police brutality following the murder of George Floyd. Many Christians left their churches because of their pastors' perceived apathy in not providing pastoral guidance or wisdom on Sunday morning concerning the horrendous event that consumed households worldwide. This was the kind of injury that caused Black and brown families to seek the balm and blessings of God's Word. In too many churches, they found no balm and no blessings. Pastors can seize these moments to unify the congregation and to offer love, healing, and grace to families most concerned and affected by these social sins. Pastors and preachers should address national and community crises as soon as possible. The longer the wait, the sooner fear, doubt, disappointment, anger, and misinformation have time to set in within the hearts of those affected most. The time is always right to preach a word of hope when there is an immediate, well-known, and widespread crisis.

National disasters, such as tornadoes, hurricanes, wildfires, and earthquakes are crises that have the potential to rally communities together in ways that transcend racial, political, economic, and social differences when addressed immediately. Sermons that focus on unity, hope, strength in Christ, the sovereignty of God, and faith can accomplish much to galvanize congregations and strengthen individuals. Preachers can address such crises promptly because they don't need to navigate social land mines. Most of the time, preaching that addresses the human devastation and loss from natural disasters does not aim to identify people, political parties, or social systems as culprits. These crises can affect all people. Everyone desires direction and encouragement in these times of crisis.

Congregational Involvement and Timing

On April 27, 2011, the deadliest tornado in Alabama history barreled through the state. In Tuscaloosa County, the tornado took the lives of fifty-three people. Immediately following the destruction, my congregation sprung into action by taking bottles of water to the Tuscaloosa police officers working around the clock and the National Guard members called to assist in the rescue efforts. A few days later, our members gathered at the church and took two vans to a local housing project that had been completely leveled, to help with recovery efforts. Upon returning to the church, after searching and serving for close to five hours, our members' faces showed exhaustion, pain, disappointment, and hopelessness. Some were weeping. Others were utterly silent. After hearing the report of search crews finding the remains of a young girl at that same site where they had volunteered, we prayed and left. There was not a person in our congregation that this tornado had not touched directly or indirectly. My own daughter and son-in-law lost their home and narrowly escaped physical harm. They took cover in the bathtub, as the EF5 tornado, with its freight-train howl, blasted through their subdivision.

President Obama visited Tuscaloosa on April 29, 2011, to survey the damage before signing an emergency declaration for the state of Alabama that summoned aid from the Federal Emergency Management Agency (FEMA).[4] The tornado of April 27, 2011, would be a defining moment for our congregation. Preaching to a congregation affected by the tornado developed a deeper social consciousness for them.

The Sunday after the tornado's deadly destruction, I preached a message entitled "Strength of Hope." The timing was right. There was both a spiritual and social crisis. People were hurt and without homes, some without insurance or assurance. Many had no place to go. People wondered if there was a word from the Lord. It would have been irresponsible and a dereliction of my pastoral obligation if I had not addressed the devastation of April 27 in my sermon. One of the factors that made it easy for me to address a social crisis from the pulpit so soon after the tornado was our congregation's involvement in the life of our community. Our church's motto is "Christ Committed, Community Connected." Although this crisis had a deep impact on our congregation, it was not the first time we were actively involved with a community crisis caused by a natural disaster.

In 2005, hundreds of New Orleans' residents flooded Tuscaloosa County. Many found shelter at the University of Alabama and the Bowers Park gymnasium. Our mission and outreach ministry joined

---

4. The Tuscaloosa News, *Eye of the Storm: The Devastation, Resiliency and Restoration of Tuscaloosa, Alabama,* (Canada: Pediment Publishing, 2011), 34–35.

a host of agencies, churches, and organizations to provide food, cloth-ing, and overnight shelter for these image-bearers forced to flee their homes. As a result of our congregational involvement, two families from New Orleans joined our church, after deciding to remain and call Tuscaloosa their new home. For churches regularly involved in social crisis ministry, the social crisis sermon is embraced and expected, making timing less of a sensitive issue.

Some churches long to reflect and express the love of Christ in the day-to-day realities that face humanity. Social involvement is a form of Christian discipleship for these churches, and is even factored into their annual budgets. These congregations give to agencies like the United Negro College Fund, Southern Christian Leadership Conference, Moth-ers Against Drunk Driving, Destiny Rescue, National Alliance to End Homelessness, Habitat for Humanity, and other socially active agencies. For these congregations, social crisis preaching is frequent, because they have ministries and resources ready to address social crises and injustices in their communities. Most likely, these churches are members of faith traditions or denominations where social involvement is the norm. Social crisis preaching may need to be more frequent in these local bodies, since the congregation views social involvement as a discipline of ser-vice and, therefore, part of their spiritual development and formation.

Pastors who preach weekly may include frequent social crisis ser-mons as part of the discipleship program. They may also challenge the congregation through relevant application in the sermon. Even these congregations need to be fed sermons from various genres and books of the Bible so that they will be spiritually nourished. Thus, every area of their personal lives will manifest Christian witness for the glory of God.

Then there are congregations where worship, liturgy, and practicing ordinances are priorities in the life of the denomination, church, and its members. For these churches, social and civic engagement have not been a part of the church. Members of these churches may not vote in local and national elections at all, and voter registration drives are nonexistent. While it is possible in these churches for preaching to be spread out among biblical genres, the congregation does not view social involve-ment as part of the spiritual development curriculum of the church.

The above examples of two different kinds of churches represent two extremes. Both churches need more balance in their sermon offerings.

The first needs to hear sermons that encourage spiritual formation and renewal, because any church that is highly involved in social crisis ministry and civic engagement must have spiritually mature members for those ministries to be effective and for the church to maintain a theologically healthy posture. The second church, however, needs to be challenged to self-denial, cross-bearing, and sacrificial service because any church disengaged from the day-to-day matters, social ills, and political corruption that affects the membership is forfeiting opportunities to be the salt of the earth and the light of the world (Matthew 5). Proctor shares wisdom on the issue:

> Are we going to preach only to crisis situations that are imposed on us by the media and the protagonist in the streets, or will we identify a few of the priority needs of the community and keep them before the people, to raise their consciousness, to provide support for agencies that deal with such priorities, and to give integrity to the work that we do for God as a herald of the good news?[5]

Balance and consistency in the pulpit will ensure that the church is balanced and consistent in its spiritual and social practices. This is the healthiest model, and the church that will serve our neighbors well and glorify God to the highest degree.

Timing and Ongoing Crisis

The social aftermath of the tornado of April 27 created greater involvement for our members and ministries. It exposed a myriad of social concerns in our community. It revealed the lack of affordable housing, rogue landlord practices, and the lack of healthcare, raising anxiety about which community would receive aid and restoration first and which would have to wait. Some are still waiting. The point here is clear. Some crises are of such magnitude that the timing to address them in the sermon is immediate. But then, for some communities, there are other crises that never end.

[5.] Samuel D. Proctor, *Preaching about Crises in the Community* (Philadelphia: Westminster, 1988), 91.

Some crises can unearth social inequities, communal and familial dysfunction, economic injustice, and opportunity disparities that have been lying beneath the surface. In August 2005, Category-five Hurricane Katrina decimated New Orleans. Although the hurricane ransacked New Orleans, the overwhelmingly Black community from the Lower Ninth Ward felt the most brutal brunt of the devastation.

As news channels plastered 24–hour coverage of the aftermath, it was the bereft, hopeless, and desperate images of the overwhelming number of African Americans seeking shelter at the New Orleans Superdome that shined light on a plethora of racial injustices and inequities. Why was there such an overrepresentation of African Americans left without homes and shelter? Why wasn't the response from the government swift and sufficient? Such questions stare in the faces of both the agents of secular government and the sacred ambassadors of the kingdom of God. Although Hurricane Katrina did not happen in Tuscaloosa, the people of New Orleans are our neighbors, and some of them became our family. Preaching that addresses the social pain of our members and their neighbors is a Christian responsibility that proclaimers of the gospel must bear.

While there is the need to preach a word of hope immediately for crises such as natural disasters, there also is a need to address the lingering social crises that remain long after the winds and rains have passed. The timing of addressing these issues must be considered with wisdom and taking into account a host of practical concerns.

When the preacher is conscious of social crises in the community and the world, consistent social crisis preaching ensures that the congregation's consciousness is also tuned in to the hurts and hopes of other people. No congregation can afford to become "lovers of self, lovers of money, boastful, proud, demeaning" (2 Tim 3:2). Without a constant reminder that we are our brother's and sister's keeper, Christians will turn inward, and the spirit of individualism can easily occupy the heart. It should be our resolve to "carry one another's burdens" (Gal 6:2). Consistency in social crisis preaching helps to prevent faddish and bandwagon preaching.

Some preachers preach on social issues because it is trendy or because everyone else is doing it. Some submit to the pressure to be popular and to join the proclamation bandwagon to stay relevant or popular with their parishioners. Avoid this practice at all costs. The pulpit is not a stage for popularity seekers. When preachers are consistent, they don't have to cave to pressures to remain popular. Social crisis preaching is a part of their homiletical DNA.

Similarly, when there is consistency in social crisis preaching, preachers avoid the pressures of speaking on a particular social issue at a very sensitive time in the congregation's life. For instance, if a member or member's relative was recently arrested, a sermon on the problems of crime and rising crime statistics could be perceived as a personal attack, or that the pastor is meddling. With social crisis preaching there is such a thing as bad timing. But when the congregation is accustomed to hearing messages that keep social issues and systemic injustices before the people, the sermon will be viewed with less suspicion, even if it is scheduled at a sensitive time.

In addition to allowing the text to speak to relevant social crises on the regular preaching calendar, I recommend that preachers devote a sermon every quarter to intentionally confront an ongoing national or communal social crisis (e.g., Matt 26:11). An intentional calendar could look like this:

Quarter 1 – Genesis 1:27 – "Roots of Racism"
Quarter 2 – Revelation 7 –"Racism in 'Our' World"
Quarter 3 – Acts 10:1–35 – "Racism in Our Heart"
Quarter 4 – Colossians 3:11 – "Racism in the Church"

Or

Quarter 1 – Suicide: Acts 16:25–28 – "Don't Do It, We Are Here!"[6]
Quarter 2 – Immigration: Leviticus 19:33–34 – "Won't You Be My Neighbor?"
Quarter 3 – Poverty: James 5:1–6 – "The Haves and the Have-Nots"
Quarter 4 – Family: Ephesians 5:22–6:4 – "Family Matters"

A pastor must weigh the frequency of the social crisis preaching calendar against the congregation's involvement (consistent preaching

---

[6.] This sermon was preached at Plum Grove Baptist Church on August 15, 2021, by Rev. Corey Savage, executive pastor, to address mental health.

will increase this) and their needs, with discernment from the Holy Spirit.

While delivery considerations focus on the timing and balance of the sermon, a complimentary aspect is the rhetorical concerns. As stated before, the purpose of delivery considerations is to enable the preacher to grip and sustain the congregation's attention by preaching captivating sermons that also aid in their much-needed spiritual formation. All preachers, without forethought, and in varying degrees, use the three modes of persuasion: *ethos* (ethics), *logos* (logic), and *pathos* (passion). When the Holy Spirit is the fuel of our preaching, these rhetorical concerns provide strength and character to the social crisis sermon.

RHETORICAL CONCERNS: DELIVERY

One of the dangers of social crisis preaching is the possibility that people could perceive it as a political or social speech. Whenever rhetoric is misplaced or misused, it can become manipulative and used as a tool for anything other than Christian discipleship. Rhetoric is present—effectively or ineffectively—in every form of public speaking. When we use the term *rhetoric*, Greek or Roman orators usually come to mind. In my research, I have investigated the similarities and differences between ancient Greek oratory and Christian proclamation. Rhetoric was not strictly limited to the most educated or secular thinkers and speakers. In my previous work, I note how Quintilian disagreed with Cicero that rhetoric belonged to the educated elite.[7] Quintilian argued that every speaker, regardless of socioeconomic status, possesses the ability to persuade (rhetoric), when he argues,

> Cicero, it is true, attributed the origin of oratory to founders of cities and legislators, who must indeed have possessed the power of speech. But I do not see why he makes this the actual origin, because there are nomadic peoples even today who have no cities

---

[7.] The research on Greco-Roman oratory and Christian proclamation, and Paul's theology of proclamation was taken from my own work in my PhD dissertation on social crisis preaching. See Tyshawn Gardner, "An Analysis of Prophetic Radicalism in the Social Crisis Preaching of Kelly Miller Smith, Sr." (PhD diss., Southern Baptist Theological Seminary, 2019), chap. 3.

or laws, and yet people born among them act as ambassadors, prosecute and defend, and, indeed, think that some people are better speakers than others.[8]

New Testament writings were so intensely imbued with rhetoric that, according to Duane Litfin, "this pervasive rhetorical tradition was a prime ingredient in the cultural heritage that defined the Greco-Roman world and gave the ancient mind its shape. The people thrived on eloquence and treated its practitioners as celebrities."[9] Laurent Pernot suggests, "Contrary to a commonly held view . . . that associates rhetoric with the idea of manipulating others' minds, antiquity located rhetoric closer to debate and exchange and bound it up with freedom of expression in the search for persuasion and deliberation in common."[10] Here is where Christian rhetoric in preaching is decisively distinct from rhetoric employed by public speakers, politicians, and lawyers. Although each of these professions, including preaching, has a goal to persuade, preachers are not mere public speakers. Instead, Christian preachers submit to the dictates of the Holy Spirit and are governed by the fruit of the Spirit.

Early Christian proclamation and ancient Greco-Roman rhetoric were similar in function but entirely different in motive. Whereas the Greco-Roman rhetor focused on persuasion by the power of rhetoric, Christian proclamation focuses on transforming the heart by the power of the Holy Spirit. Pernot suggests, "It is essential . . . to see clearly that for a long time nothing walled off paganism from Christianity concerning rhetoric. Some Christian orators were students of pagan rhetors."[11] The most notable of Christian proclaimers influenced by Greco-Roman rhetoric was St. Augustine of Hippo.

As a student and teacher of rhetoric, Augustine confesses, "At a vulnerable age I was to study the textbooks on eloquence. I wanted to distinguish myself as an orator for a damnable and conceited purpose,

---

[8.] Quintilian, *The Orator's Education*, Books 3–5, ed. and trans. Donald A. Russell (Cambridge, MA: Harvard University, 2001), 23.
[9.] Duane Litfin, *Paul's Theology of Preaching: The Apostle's Challenge to the Art of Persuasion in Ancient Corinth* (Downers Grove, IL: IVP, 2015), 57–58.
[10.] Laurent Pernot, *Rhetoric in Antiquity*, trans. W. E. Higgins (Washington, DC: Catholic University of America, 2005), 202.
[11.] Pernot, 207.

namely delight in human vanity."[12] Some of the most eloquent Christians in the early church were trained in the art of rhetoric. Among them, according to Pernot, was "a line of truly great names . . . sheds luster on Christian rhetoric. In Greek, there were Eusebius of Caesarea; the Cappadocian Fathers, Gregory of Nazianzus, called 'Christian Demosthenes,' Gregory of Nyssa, and Basil of Caesarea, and John Chrysostom."[13] Likewise, there are eloquent preachers in our age who use powerful rhetorical tools in their social crisis sermons, like Robert Smith, Jr., Ralph Douglas West, J.D. Greear, Russell Moore, Doug Webster, Emil Thomas, J. Alfred Smith, Charlie Dates, Matt Adair, and many others.

Preachers from Jesus and Paul to expositors in the present era are called to preach the Word of the Lord with authority, spiritual precision, and uncompromising integrity. The apostle Paul's theology of preaching, which also bears Paul's convictions about Greco-Roman rhetoric, is best seen in the first four chapters of 1 Corinthians. Paul could not escape the use of rhetoric, nor did he try. Litfin states, "Paul was forced by the situation in Corinth to explain and defend his *modus operandi* (mode of operation) as a preacher."[14] While ancient orators were motivated to obtain results by their own strength and resources, Paul's motive was rooted in faithfulness to the God who was responsible for the increase of his labor (1 Cor 3:6). Paul was a herald with motives entirely distinct from that of the ancient orator; however, Paul does use a variety of rhetorical strategies to reach his audience. For instance, in Acts 14 he appeals to Jewish history, but in Acts 17 at the Areopagus, Paul contextualizes his message and uses the content of Greek poets to explain the true and living God.

Most importantly for Paul, the power of his speech was not in his words, but rather in the power of the Spirit (1 Cor 1:17, 2:1–5). Paul did not depend upon mere words, nor did he try to appease or impress his hearers by his eloquence. The Corinthians chided him on his elementary speech, unpleasant appearance, and lack of eloquence in presentation (2 Cor 11:6). Paul did, in fact, use the available means

---

[12.] Saint Augustine, *Saint Augustine Confessions*, trans. Henry Chadwick (Oxford: Oxford University, 2009), 38.

[13.] Pernot, 206–7.

[14.] Litfin, 141.

of persuasion. A picture of his rhetorical strategy is found in 1 Thess 1:5. He writes, "Our gospel came to you not only in word [logos], but also in power and in the Holy Spirit and with full conviction [pathos] (ESV). You know what kind of men we proved to be among you for your sake [ethos]." Like the ancient orator, Paul wanted desperately to persuade men. He was aware of the culture's desire for appealing, amusing speech, but he was more concerned with pointing his hearers beyond himself and towards Jesus Christ. Similarly, social crisis preaching exalts the justice of God by proclaiming spiritual and social liberation through the power of the gospel of Jesus Christ. The gospel and spiritual power that deliver us from spiritual death are the same gospel and spiritual power that can break the strongholds of the systems and structures that relegate God's creation to the margins of society.

Aristotle's three modes of persuasion, *ethos*, *logos*, and *pathos*, contribute key ingredients to the classical rhetoric used in social crisis preaching. In ancient Greece, the orator's rhetorical understanding was measured by their possession and use of *ethos*, *logos*, and *pathos*. The rhetor's *ethos* is a testament to their moral fiber and perceived character. *Logos* has to do with logic, the speaker's ability to reason. Finally, *pathos* is measured by the orator's passion and emotional appeal, as well as their ability to stir the passion of the listeners. Since social crisis preaching aims to persuade congregations to "intentionally care about and confront the crises in their neighbor's community in the power of the Holy Spirit," it is essential that a brief discussion takes place here about the role of the modes of persuasion in social crisis preaching.

Ethos: Social Crisis Preaching and Pastoral Ethics

High-profile social crises are often the consequence of the decisions of unethical people. *Ethos* pertains to the ethics of the preacher, meaning their perceived character. With a vast swath of opinions circulating on some of our contemporary social crises, it is very easy to slip into the trend of weighing in on these issues for the wrong reasons. My definition of social crisis preaching, "Biblically rooted, Spirit-enabled proclamation that develops and drives congregations to compassionately care for and radically confront the social crisis in the communities where their neighbors live, work, worship, and play," has a pastoral responsibility tethered to it: social crisis preaching develops faithful disciples for Christ. The lure of faddish preaching to gain more social media likes, conference appearances, and large honorariums can be tempting. But the preacher serving in the role of prophet must not concern themselves with profits.

Preachers must have clear, ethical motives. They have become the secret weapon of political and social action groups on all sides, targeted to endorse political and cultural messages to win the vote and the favor of the captive audiences that show up in our pews and social media platforms. There is no wonder that many preachers, some for good reasons, become politicians. But the herald, who is ethical and committed to the cause of Christ, cannot be bought, bossed, or bullied into becoming corporate cosigners or building agendas for political partners or ecclesiastical entities.

What does ethics have to do with social crisis delivery considerations? Preachers whose lives reflect the gospel, and who have an ethical or social message, are given undivided attention before they even read the text from the pulpit. How do we measure this ethical quality? One way is our willingness to suffer. Preaching is strengthened by a life that practices what we preach. Christlikeness in pastoral practice includes walking the path of him who "took up our pain, and bore our suffering" (Isa 53:4a NIV). We are called to take up our cross and follow Christ (Matt 10:38), because Peter admonishes, "To this you were called, because Christ suffered for you, leaving you an example, that you should follow in his steps" (1 Pet 2:21 NIV). As pastors consider sermonic delivery, they must also consider ethical demonstration.

Even a surface survey of preachers known for their social crisis sermons will show that, although they were not perfect, they held to an ethical standard by their willingness to forego personal luxuries and to stand with the suffering and downtrodden. These preachers often paid an enormous personal cost. Martin Luther King, Jr., Dietrich Bonhoeffer, Helmut Thielicke, Fred Shuttlesworth, James Earl Massey, Wyatt Tee Walker, and John Perkins, to name a few, withstood denominational backlash, the silence of fellow clergy, and the abuse of nations to be faithful to God and to suffer with the suffering. Ethics undergirds sermonic delivery.

Logos: Truth and Facts in the Social Crisis Sermon

On July 10, 2015, thirty-five-year-old Anthony Ware died in the custody of the Tuscaloosa Police Department (TPD). With the very high-profile and controversial police shooting that caused the death of Michael Brown in August 2014, emotions, mistrust, fear, and caution remained high across the country. Soon after the news broke of Ware's killing, I called for a meeting with our mayor, police chief, and local pastors. Based on the news reports, I was angry and disappointed going into the meeting, that the entire incident had not been captured on body camera.[15]

During the meeting, Steve Anderson, the current police chief, said that not every officer had body cameras. He explained the enormous price of the cameras, as well as the cost of the data to keep them running. Anderson provided details of the TPD budget, the number of officers who had body cameras, and his aggressive efforts to outfit every TPD officer with a camera.

While the death of a Black man at the hands of a police officer was still an event that caused tension, suspicion, and hurt, one of the factors at the center of the uproar—the lack of body-camera evidence and transparency—was dispelled due to the conversation that several pastors and I had with the chief of police. Obtaining correct information from a credible and reliable source is critical in assuaging some of the suspicion and lack of transparency around an issue. I was able to speak to other key leaders and Mr. Ware's family about the truth concerning some of the procedures in police arrest, particularly that of the Ware arrest. Today, every TPD officer wears a body camera that is on and always operating. Going into that meeting, I was armed with assumptions, not correct answers, and several falsehoods, not facts. Had I given a sermon based on that false information, it could have produced an irreconcilable moment between our community and the TPD.

Sound and clear reasoning involves obtaining the correct information

---

15. Haley Townsend, "Raw Footage from Anthony Ware death in police custody," *CBS42*, July 15, 2015, https://www.cbs42.com/news/local/raw-footage-from-anthony-ware-death-in-police-custody/. This article contains the details of the Ware arrest, death, and the explanation Chief Anderson provided concerning why the entire incident was not on body camera. Anderson's statement to this news outlet is also consistent with the conversation he and Mayor Walt Maddox had with me and the ministers after the incident.

and presenting it responsibly. To persuade listeners to care about and confront the crises in their neighbor's community, social crisis preachers must be girded with the truth of the Word of God and the correct facts about the matters they are addressing.

Raymond Bailey provides compelling and noteworthy advice concerning this matter by highlighting two weaknesses that render sermons ineffective and untrustworthy. Of "glittering generalities," Bailey states, "there is the broad statement that makes undocumented accusations and sweeping promises that go beyond the Scriptures."[16] General statements, poorly researched, secondhand information, and unclear, vague assertions undermine the power and persuasibility of the social crisis sermon. Preachers who speak in generalities amid critical matters do a disservice towards the cause they are representing.

The "glittering generalities" are a sign of laziness and dishonesty. Presenting correct facts often requires the sweat and labor of deep research—listening and reading. Some matters are too important for preachers to "guesstimate" (or quickly Google search). Generalities create strife, division, and opinionated hostilities. They do not inspire passion, stir the conscience, provoke interest, or motivate action like clear, indisputable facts. Generalizations misrepresent people and thwart opportunities for collaborative work and reconciliation.

For instance, the legacy and words of King are often hijacked by groups who are only familiar with small sections of his "I Have a Dream" speech.[17] Portions of this speech indeed call for unity and paint a beautiful picture of the Beloved Community. But not everyone uses the segment of this speech (or other King speeches) where he calls attention to the reasons we don't have a beloved community. The attempt to cite, even to cite correctly, notable and famous personalities to win congregations over to a particular position is unwise. The well-disciplined congregation is always fact-checking, researching, and most importantly, asking the right questions. Misrepresentation of facts and partial truth will hurt the preacher's chances of being heard in the future. When people of goodwill are given facts, bridges

---

[16.] Raymond Bailey, "Ethics in Preaching," in *Handbook of Contemporary Preaching: A Wealth of Counsel for Creative and Effective Proclamation*, ed. Michael Duduit (Nashville: B&H, 1992), 555.

[17.] Martin Luther King, Jr., *A Call to Conscience: The Landmark Speeches of Dr. Martin Luther King, Jr.* Edited by Clayborn Carson and Kris Shepard, (New York: Warner 2001), Kindle, 80–86.

of understanding are built, and the progress of reconciliation and cor-
recting injustices can begin.

Pathos: With Head and Heart

On a beautiful day in the Fall 1997 semester as a religion major at
Samford University and a part of the H-Day program,[18] I stopped by
Professor James Barnette's office in Chapman Hall. As we spoke, I could
not keep my eyes off the portrait on his office wall. It showed King
and a gentleman whom I would later find out was Professor Barnette's
father, Dr. Henlee Barnette. King and Barnette looked as if they had
just finished dining. King's tie was loose, the top button on his shirt
unbuttoned, and both men looked casual and relaxed.

I asked Professor Barnette about the picture. He replied, "That's
Dr. King and my dad, immediately after Dr. King held an audience at the Southern Baptist Theological Seminary spellbound for
an hour."[19] Professor Barnette continued to tell me that his father,
and some of the professors and administrators at Southern, asked
King about the possibility of him teaching there. King's reply was
one of a man consumed with a passion he could not avoid or deny.
He spoke as one possessing a burning passion that could not be
exchanged for any opportunity—no matter how prestigious, lucra-
tive, or comfortable. King simply replied, "Thank you, but I have
a calling to fulfill."

Social crisis preaching cannot exist without calling. The burden is
too heavy; the risk is too dangerous; the pay is too small; and the appreciation is sometimes nonexistent for any preacher to commit to.
A divine calling is what generates and funds a social crisis preacher.
It also means that the preacher ought to deliver passionate sermons.
Why? As chapter 2 illustrated, God cares for and confronts social issues;
therefore, the preacher has been commissioned by God to passionately

---

[18.] H-Day is now referred to as Samford Sunday. It is a program designed to connect Samford
student preachers to Alabama Baptist pastors by allowing them opportunities to gain experience in
preaching on Sunday mornings. See https://www.samford.edu/programs/samford-sunday.

[19.] From a conversation with the late Dr. James Barnette in 1997 at Samford University. See
description of the King visit as detailed by Dr. Henlee Barnette, *The Southern Baptist Theological
Seminary*, "Dr. King's Visit," From Barnette's: *The Visit of Martin Luther King, Jr., Part Two, Review
and Expositor*," https://archives.sbts.edu/the-history-of-the-sbts/our-lore/dr-kings-visit/.

invest himself in caring for and confronting social crisis issues in his neighborhood. Passionate sermons reiterate to congregations that they too need to be personally invested and compassionately active.

Passion and Personal Investment

Passions stem from personal investment. Some people just like to preach. They love the art of preaching, the challenge of parsing verbs and uncovering meaning in the text. Some preachers love the thrill of the call and response. Some just love preaching. Passion not only sustains preaching but also supports the work that the preaching calls them to. Some topics stir my emotions, move my heart, and make me angry. There are some social crises I care about deeply but in which I may not have a personal investment. On the other hand, there are other social crises I care about and do have a deep personal investment in.

Personal investment is measured in time, treasure, and tears. I am personally invested in racial justice equity because I have given over twenty years of my life and ministry to it, serving communities that have borne the brunt of injustice and neglect. I've served three years as the president of the Tuscaloosa chapter of the Southern Christian Leadership Conference. I have led justice rallies in my city, challenged local school system administration, met with Black and white pastors to bridge understanding of splintered communities, and worked tirelessly and successfully with my church family to fight liquor stores coming into our community. I've spent countless hours with individuals and families whose names will never be known, because they needed someone to stand with them when their child was being unfairly expelled or their family evicted by a rogue landlord. Nothing spells investment like time.

Tears have been shed. I have a brother who is currently incarcerated, and I have personally experienced the pain and frustration created when young adults make bad decisions, compounded by a merciless and unyielding criminal justice system. I've watched parents cry because their child did not make parole, and I've cried with children because their parents would not be home for holidays or graduation. Personal investment is also measured in the investment of one's treasure. One example is our congregation's mission giving to address the adverse impact of the cash bail system on communities of color. People who cannot post bail are often subject to long jail stays for nonviolent crimes, greatly decreasing their chances to work and care for their families. The giving of one's resources is one of the most sacrificial acts of Christian discipleship. Giving to causes that align with God's redemptive purposes can be liberating, freeing, and a rejection of the spirit of materialism. Being personally invested in the giving of one's time, shedding of one's tears, and contributing of one's treasure is indeed a pre-proclamation function of the social crisis preacher. These personal investments precede the crisis proclamation and are witnessed in the passion with which the preacher delivers the social crisis message.

Unless there is a personal investment in the subject, social crisis preaching cannot be sustained. The prophet's call was a call to be personally invested. Moses's call was made known to him by a burning bush that kept burning (Exod 3:1–4). His investment was demonstrated in his suffering and sacrifice with and for the people of Israel, "No prophet has arisen again in Israel like Moses, whom the LORD knew face to face. He was unparalleled for all the signs and wonders the LORD sent him to do against the land of Egypt—to Pharaoh, to all his officials, and to all his land—and for all the mighty acts of power and terrifying deeds that Moses performed in the sight of all Israel" (Deut 34:10–12).

Consider Hosea's deep call into personal investment: "Go take to yourself a wife of whoredom and have children of whoredom, for the land commits great whoredom by forsaking the LORD" (Hos 1:2 ESV). That's personal investment. What else can be said about the personal investment of Jeremiah when he sighed, "Oh that my head were waters, and my eyes a fountain of tears, that I might weep day and night for the slain of the daughter of my people! Oh that I had in the desert a travelers' lodging place, that I might leave my people and go away from them!" (Jer 9:1–2a ESV). Then he punctuated his personal investment by commenting, "If I say, 'I will not mention him or speak any more in his name,' there is in my heart as it were a burning fire shut up in my bones, and I am weary with holding it in, and I cannot" (Jer 20:9 ESV). A burning fire—sustained, continuous, never-ending passion shut up in his bones! Passion sustained through personal investment.

A Passion That Leads to Activism

Ben Witherington III defines *pathos* as "the stronger feelings such as anger, fear, and pity."[20] These feelings, says Witherington, are "what the rhetor hoped to arouse in the audience."[21] Sermons should arouse emotions. How does one preach about the horrors of the sex slave industry without leading the congregation to experience the kind of empathy that causes anger, fear, and, sadness, as if one of our own children was the one snatched from us? But preaching aimed at stirring the emotions alone is not the goal. The goal is to anchor the social crisis to an ethical principle within the preaching text, then to stimulate the mind with the truth derived from the text and the facts surrounding the crisis. The emotions will then be stirred to the point of sustainable, responsible, and Christlike activism. When the social crisis sermon is delivered, passion arises from an appeal to action.

Sermons that are apologetically appealing and symmetric in form, generating rational arguments crafted in logical language, may stimulate the mind, but may fail to warm the heart and motivate the hearer into "caring and confronting the crisis in our neighbor's community." In its varying forms and methods, social crisis preaching demands that the *pathos* within the hearer be stirred to action and application in the power of the Spirit. Social crisis preaching also requires that the preacher possess the *pathos* to adequately persuade the hearer.

The forces that produce injustice are supernatural; therefore, the forces that must contend with the evils that produce injustice must likewise be supernatural. Social crisis preachers understand that effective activism entails more than intellectual muscle, massive numbers, and political alliances. Paul makes this fact very clear: "For we do not wrestle against flesh and blood, but against the rulers, against the authorities, against the cosmic powers over this present darkness, against the spiritual forces of evil in the heavenly places" (Eph 6:12 ESV). Paul then explains that to contend with spiritual evil, the Christian must "take up the whole armor of God, that you may be able to withstand in the evil day" (Eph 6:13a ESV). One could not withstand the powerful,

---

[20.] Ben Witherington III, *Conflict & Community in Corinth: A Socio-Rhetorical Commentary on 1 and 2 Corinthians* (Grand Rapids: Eerdmans, 1995), 43.

[21.] Witherington III, 44.

oppressive supernatural forces of evil without being grounded and propelled by a power greater than natural strength and willpower. For Paul, to engage in this spiritual warfare, the Christian was required to "take the helmet of salvation, and the sword of the Spirit, which is the word of God, praying at all times in the Spirit, with all prayer and supplication" (Eph 6:17–18a ESV). When sermon delivery contains passion that motivates the congregation into appropriate and sacrificial social activism, preaching will develop congregations to care about and confront the social crises in their neighbor's community in the power of the Holy Spirit.

CONCLUSION

The preacher's wisdom with consideration to timing and rhetorical devices is essential in communicating the redemptive power of the cross and its relevance to social crisis. Paul's homiletical approach in his letter to the believers at Ephesus is a pristine example of balance, timing, and the use of rhetorical devices. Pastors earn the right to speak prophetically to their congregations by demonstrating the love of Christ towards those who hear their sermons. Paul establishes his care and concern for the Ephesians before he chides them about their bias and division (1:16). Paul sets the stage for challenging them towards social action by first reminding them of who they are: "He chose us in him before the foundation of the world," and giving them God's expectations for them in light of their identity: "that we should be holy and blameless before him" (Eph 1:4a ESV). Spiritually, they are seated with him in the heavenly places in Christ Jesus (Eph 2:6b). Socially, they are "created in Christ Jesus for good works" (Eph 2:10b ESV). In this sense, the spiritual and the social interpenetrate. Paul's timing is best seen in how he moves from informing the Ephesians of their Christian identity, then reminding them of how their identity translates into social realities. Next, he chides them about their social and ethnic division, and finally, he explains how God has reconciled Jews and Gentiles in one body through the cross.

Paul's use of rhetorical devices demonstrates his ability to rationally inform the Ephesians of their identity, passionately preach about the destruction of the dividing wall of hostility, and call for an ethic of unity among a once-divided people. Preaching about the reconciling event of the cross, Paul passionately (*pathos*) persuades (*logos*) the Ephesians by calling them towards Christian unity (*ethos*).

CHAPTER 5:

SOCIAL CRISIS PREACHING WITH THE MASTERS

In this chapter, we will examine three preachers—Kelly Miller Smith, Sr., Samuel DeWitt Proctor, Helmut Thielicke—who serve as exemplars of social crisis preachers. Their preaching ministries had significant social impact, particularly in the times of "social upheaval and stress"[1] that were present for the duration of their ministries. At the height of their ministries, Smith, Proctor, and Thielicke confronted poverty, racism, war, and national pride in their preaching and pastoral engagement.

There are three common characteristics that these preachers share. First, they were academics. They added significant contributions to the academy, especially in homiletics, lectures in Christian theological ethics, and writing. All three had the distinction of being theology professors and serving as key university administrators. Although other notable figures from various traditions could easily fit this mold, our three models have earned the respect of a national, intergenerational, cross-cultural, and cross-denominational audience.

Second, and principally, they were pastors. In that role these men consistently fulfilled my definition of social crisis preaching; they would regularly "engage in Christian proclamation that developed their congregation to intentionally care about and confront the social crisis in their neighbor's community in the power of the Holy Spirit." They consistently preached, discipled, cared for, and lived through social crises with their congregations as a shepherd of God's flock. As

---

[1.] Smith, Sr., *Social Crisis Preaching*, 33 (see intro., n. 10).

we will see below, they embody the five characteristics of the sacred anthropologist.

Third, true to my definition of social crisis preaching, these pastors are known for preaching amid social crises. Many celebrate Smith, Sr., Proctor, and Thielicke as three of the most prolific Christian preachers and thinkers of their respective eras. Each is known for infusing their sermons with ethical calls to embrace biblical fidelity, Trinitarian theology, and practical application. Though credentialed and accomplished scholars, each possessed the ability and willingness to communicate and identify with the masses. Smith, Sr.'s pre-proclamation functionality of the preacher would be the express characteristic of each of these men. Smith, Sr. defines pre-proclamation functionality as "what the function of the preacher has been prior to the crisis proclamation."[2] Smith, Sr., Proctor, and Thielicke were deeply engaged with the current affairs and crises affecting the lives of those they were called to serve. Smith, Sr. continues about the pre-proclamation function by stating, "Communication actually begins not when the text and title are announced, but when the minister functions in the community in relation to critical social circumstances and shows social sensitivity prior to proclamation."[3] Their preaching challenged earthly kingdoms, called the church to sobering self-examination, and inspired hope in the living Christ.

As with the biblical prophets, one of the most daring displays of social crisis preaching is confronting the corruption, sin, and injustice in national politics. These preachers addressed the crises in their own country, facing powerful, influential, and wealthy people, and articulating meaningful and effective applications to those who hear the sermon. Smith, Sr. Proctor, and Thielicke stood as exemplars of this function.

BIOGRAPHICAL SKETCHES

The birth, social background, and life formation of Smith, Sr., Proctor, and Thielicke are vitally important in understanding them as social

---

[2] Smith, Sr., 80.
[3] Smith, Sr., 81.

crisis preachers and models for social crisis preaching. While these biographical sketches are not exhaustive, they serve to inform us how these preachers were shaped and influenced. Social crisis preachers are not simply effective communicators. They are faithful Christian disciples. Smith, Sr., Proctor, and Thielicke have exemplified what it means to model life in the Spirit.

Additionally, as seen in their faithfulness to the Word of God and their intolerance of injustice and corruption in their nation's government, each of these men had to summon tremendous courage. They often paid a heavy price in their personal and professional careers for their uncompromising commitment to truth and justice. Their pulpits were not only in their churches, but their message was proclaimed from the classroom lectern, with the pen, and through the technological channels available to them through radio and television interviews.

Kelly Miller Smith, Sr.[4]

Smith, Sr. was born October 28, 1920, to Perry and Priscilla Anderson Smith in Mound Bayou, Mississippi. Smith, Sr. was named after the African American intellectual Kelly Miller, dean and professor at Howard University, who argued that Black people must resist segregation to maintain their self-respect.[5] Smith, Sr. was raised in the all-Black city of Mound Bayou, a small town in the Mississippi delta, founded by Black people who had formerly run away from the dangers of racism. Smith, Sr.'s father, Perry Monroe Smith, was a solid and steady mentor to him, a well-respected leader in Mound Bayou, and the principal founder and chief administrator of the famous Taborian Hospital.[6] Smith, Sr. completed his elementary education in Mound Bayou and graduated high school at nearby Magnolia High School in

---

[4.] Excerpts of this biographical sketch were taken from my PhD dissertation on Kelly Miller Smith, Sr. See Tyshawn Gardner, "An Analysis of Prophetic Radicalism in the Social Crisis Preaching of Kelly Miller Smith, Sr.," (see chap. 3, n. 168).

[5.] Leila A. Meier, "A Different Kind of Prophet: The Role of Kelly Miller Smith in the Nashville Civil Rights Movement, 1955–1960" (MA thesis, Vanderbilt University, 1991), 2.

[6.] The greatest achievement of the Mississippi jurisdiction of the Knights and Daughters of Tabor, and the crown jewel of Mound Bayou, was the Taborian Hospital. In 1942 the founding and construction of the Taborian Hospital was in response to the lack of quality healthcare afforded to Black citizens in state and private hospitals across the country due to segregation laws under the system of Jim Crow. In the state of Mississippi, Black citizens were often denied medical attention,

Vicksburg, Mississippi. Growing up in Mound Bayou, Smith, Sr. had the unique experience of learning two competing narratives: first, that African Americans were people of profoundly deep Christian spirituality—responsible, astute, hardworking landowners; second, that those same qualities were unrecognized, unappreciated, and denied by the dominant culture around them. Mound Bayou, located in Bolivar County, is a mere forty-four miles from Money, Mississippi, the town where the nationally known murder of then fourteen-year-old Emmett Till (1955), at the hands of J. W. Milam and Roy Bryant, took place.[7]

Smith, Sr. had plans to be a professional musician when he left Mound Bayou to enroll at Tennessee State University in Nashville.[8] Smith, Sr.'s stellar academic training took place in the Historically Black Colleges and Universities (HBCU) of Tennessee State University, Morehouse College, and Howard University.[9] After Smith, Sr. received the call to the preaching ministry, he transferred to Morehouse College in Atlanta in 1940, where he double-majored in religion and music, graduating in 1942 with a bachelor's degree. Smith, Sr. joined the cavalry of Morehouse Men that included Thurman, Mordecai Johnson, and King, who were known for combating social injustice with intellectual acumen and skillful rhetoric and writing.

---

from the most minor of injuries and sicknesses, to life-threatening illness and injuries. Though closed now, the Taborian Hospital still stands in the center of the town of Mound Bayou, Mississippi.

[7.] According to current Mound Bayou mayor, Eulah Peterson, who grew up in Mound Bayou, "Since blacks could not lodge in local hotels, Till's mother, their lawyer, and several black reporters stayed in Mound Bayou during the trial of Milam and Bryant, at the home of famed physician and civil rights leader, T. R. M. Howard." Eulah Peterson, interview with author, Mound Bayou City Hall, Mound Bayou, MS, May 22, 2019.

[8.] Kelly Miller Smith, Jr., informs, "If he had not gone into the ministry, his real passion was to be a jazz musician." Kelly Miller Smith, Jr. and Alice Smith, interview with author, Griggs Hall, American Baptist College, Nashville, May 30, 2019. Also see "A Memorial to the Life and Ministry of Kelly Miller Smith, Sr." obituary, *Nashville Spotlight*, July 30, 1984, Vanderbilt University, Jean and Alexander Heard Library, Special Collections and University Archives, Kelly Miller Smith Papers, box 16, file 22.

[9.] Historically Black Colleges and Universities are institutions founded before the Civil Rights Act of 1964, and which had as their primary mission, the training of African Americans. Prior to the Civil Rights Act of 1964 (and beyond), African Americans were barred from predominantly white institutions in the US. Smith attended two of the most prestigious HBCUs in the country, Morehouse College and Howard University. *US News and World Report* ranks Howard University and Morehouse College second and fourth, respectively, as the best HBCUs in the country. Briana Boyington and Sarah Wood, "Top 10 Historically Black Colleges and Universities," *U.S. News and World Report*, February 15, 2022, accessed March 30, 2022, https://www.usnews.com/education/best-colleges/slideshows/top-10-historically-black-colleges-and-universities.

Smith, Sr.'s pastoral ministry would begin back in his home state of Mississippi at Mount Heroden Baptist Church in Vicksburg, two hours south of Mound Bayou. He was the pastor of Mount Heroden from 1946–1951. During his tenure, he launched a lifelong career in the academy, serving as dean of the religion department at Natchez College from 1946–1948.[10]

While pastoring Mount Heroden, Smith, Sr. married Alice Mae Clark, a native of Jackson, Mississippi, in 1950. Smith, Sr. left his native Mississippi in 1951 for the call of ministry at First Baptist Church, Capitol Hill in Nashville and for further work in the academies of Nashville, most notably at American Baptist Theological Seminary, and eventually for his groundbreaking work at Vanderbilt Divinity School. At American Baptist College, Smith, Sr. joined with and led an activist delegation of students that included C. T. Vivian, James M. Lawson, John Lewis, Bernard LaFayette, James Bevel, and Diane Nash, who would each later hold prominent positions on the national civil rights stage. Lewis eventually became a Representative in the United States Congress (D-GA, 1987–2020). Like Smith, Sr., each of these key individuals who served in the movement came to Nashville to pursue careers in ministry but considered activism as much a part of ministry as verbally spreading the good news.

On May 6, 1951, Smith, Sr. became the pastor of First Baptist Church, Capitol Hill. He remained there for thirty-three years until his death in 1984. In 1963, Smith, Sr. was called to become the pastor of one of the most prominent African American churches, Antioch Baptist Church in Cleveland, Ohio. But after only three months, he sensed that his work in Nashville was not complete. Since First Baptist Church, Capitol Hill had not yet chosen a successor for Smith, Sr., according to John Britton, they "voted to re-call their beloved minister, with only about 25 objections out of over 250 voting."[11] Smith, Sr.'s love for his

---

[10.] Barry Everett Lee, "The Nashville Civil Rights Movement: A Study of the Phenomenon of Intentional Leadership Development and Its Consequences for Local Movements and the National Civil Rights Movement" (PhD diss., Georgia State University, 2010), 57.

[11.] John Britton, "Why Minister Quit $1 Million Baptist Church," *Jet*, January 23, 1964, 18–26. Smith's son, Kelly Miller Smith, Jr., also recalls stories of his family's unannounced departure from Antioch Baptist Church on a Sunday morning after his father's sermon. Britton's article in *Jet* includes an interview with Smith, with questions focusing on the reason of his return to First Baptist Church, Capitol Hill. Britton states, "At Antioch, Smith presided over 2,670 members. He

Nashville church, and the unfinished business of racial reconciliation in Nashville, explains why, as Britton states, "Rev. Kelly Miller Smith, of the distinguished Mound Bayou, Miss[issippi] Smiths, was about to turn his back on a rich, prestigious Cleveland Baptist Church to return to the much smaller congregation, First Baptist."[12]

In June 1969, Walter J. Harrelson, former dean of Vanderbilt Divinity School, hired Smith, Sr. as the first African American faculty member. Smith, Sr. was appointed as assistant dean and lecturer in Church and Ministries. At Vanderbilt, Smith, Sr. established the Black Church Studies program and the first program of study in the country on prominent African American theologian and philosopher Thurman.

Smith, Sr. was recognized by *Ebony* magazine in 1954 as one of the ten most outstanding preachers in America. *Ebony* is the broadest circulated magazine of any African American publication in history. Most profoundly, Smith, Sr. is one of only twelve African Americans to give the Lyman Beecher Lectures at Yale in its almost 150–year history.[13] Smith, Sr.'s commitment to his role as pastor of First Baptist Church, Capitol Hill displayed a particular ecclesiological praxis that

---

commanded a $10,000 salary, plus $250 monthly living expenses. A 17–year-old credit union at Antioch has assets estimated at over $400,000. The edifice and all its equipment might add up to a half-million dollars, if not more. First Baptist is indeed modest in comparison. It has 450 members, no credit union, and a church valued at about $100,000." See Britton, 25–26.

12. Britton, 18.

13. Established April 12, 1871, The Lyman Beecher Lectures at Yale Divinity School are one of the most prestigious lecture series on preaching in the nation. At the request of Henry Ward Beecher, the annual lectures were to be named after his father, Lyman Beecher. At the behest of the chief donor, Henry W. Sage and the Yale Corporation, "the Lyman Beecher lecturer shall be invited to lecture on a branch of pastoral theology or any other topic appropriate to the work of the Christian ministry." Yale Divinity School, "Bibliography of the Lyman Beecher Lectureship on Preaching," accessed December 12, 2018, https://www.library.yale.edu/div/beecher.html. Among the notables to have delivered these lectures are J. A. Broadus (1888), P. T. Forsyth (1906), John Henry Jowett (1911), Reinhold Niebuhr (1944), Fred Craddock (1977), and Walter Brueggemann (1988). There are less notable names, but the sermons delivered during the 146 years of the lectures' existence are parallel in substance and scholarship. In 1949, Edgar DeWitt Jones conducted a survey of the Lyman Beecher lecturers, and within that survey he listed several categories, among which is a group that he labels "Prophets of Social Change." The distinguished preachers under that label include Washington Gladden (1886 and 1901), Henry Sloane Coffin (1917), Garfield Bromley Oxnam (1943), and Kelly Miller Smith, Sr. (1982–1983). The other African Americans to preach the Lyman Beecher Lectures are James H. Robinson (1954–1955); Henry Mitchell (1973–1974); Gardner C. Taylor (1975–1976); James Forbes (1985–1986); Samuel D. Proctor (1989–1990); Thomas Hoyt (1992–1993); Peter Gomes (1998); Otis Moss, Jr. (2004); Renita J. Weems (the only African American woman) (2008); Brian K. Blount (2011); Otis Moss III (2014). Yale Divinity School, "Bibliography of the Lyman Beecher Lectureship on Preaching."

commits evangelical Christianity to be involved with people afflicted through social crisis, thus joining the spiritual with the social. The current president at American Baptist College, Forrest Harris, states, "Smith had a great charisma and was celebrated in Nashville as one who bridged the black and white community. Kelly was the prophetic intellectual activist . . . scholar, activist, preacher."[14] Smith, Sr.'s physical stature, his baritone voice, exceptional English, and calm demeanor made him a statesman, a bridge-builder, and a trusted liaison of both Black and white communities in an age fractured with racial animosity and ecclesiastical conflict.

Samuel Dewitt Proctor

Very few pastors have had the spiritual and ministerial influence among generations of preachers and pastors as Proctor. The impact of his ministry has extended beyond his life. Proctor was a pastor, professor, Peace Corps leader, and prolific writer. In the African American preaching tradition, he ranks among the most notable and beloved. And among preachers in America, he bridged great divides in fractured human relationships in communities and churches in the United States with integrity and character.

Proctor was born July 13, 1921, in Norfolk, Virginia. He was reared in a humble and loving home his maternal grandfather built, which was the foundation of what he calls his "moral incubator."[15] Proctor's paternal grandmother was born enslaved around 1855.[16] She worked for a wealthy tobacco plantation owner, who provided her opportunities to learn to read and write. Her owner would later send her to Hampton Institute, where she would enroll and graduate in 1882.[17] Proctor's grandmother was profoundly influential to him and his siblings. She raised all eight of her own children to study beyond high

---

[14.] Forrest Harris, president, American Baptist College, interview with author, American Baptist College, Nashville, May 30, 2019.

[15.] Samuel Proctor, *Samuel Proctor: My Moral Odyssey*, 21 (see chap. 3, n. 36).

[16.] Most enslaved people never knew their exact birthdate. Few records were kept on the births and deaths of African slaves, and those records that did survive were not accessible to slaves; thus Proctor's grandmother would not have known her official age or birth date.

[17.] Adam L. Bond, *The Imposing Preacher: Samuel DeWitt Proctor and Black Public Faith* (Minneapolis: Fortress, 2013), 37.

school, a feat rarely heard of among African Americans in the early twentieth century.

Proctor's educational drive was also instilled in the home, where he and his siblings were required to learn music, poetry, and math. Despite obstacles, opposition, and systemic racial challenges, Proctor was surrounded by grandparents and parents who achieved and excelled in education. This kind of resilience amidst racial acrimony would shape Proctor's ministry and profoundly influence his preaching.

As much as education was a priority and premium in the Proctor household, the Christian faith was paramount and interlaced every aspect of their lives. Proctor's father was a Baptist church leader, his four uncles were pastors, and many of his teachers were his Sunday school teachers. From an early age, Proctor learned that three of the most potent weapons to fight injustice were faith, education, and community. A son of the Black church, Adam Bond states, "Proctor was the product of a loving home, a Baptist congregation that connected theological and racial consciousness to moral and social achievement, and a formal theological education that prepared him for his unique vocational challenges."[18]

In 1937 Proctor enrolled at and attended Virginia State College on a music scholarship, only completing a year before leaving for a career at the Norfolk Naval Yard. Heeding the call to preach, Proctor enrolled in Virginia Union University in 1940 and graduated two years later. Then Proctor enrolled as the only Black student at Crozer Theological Seminary in Pennsylvania. He graduated with a bachelor of divinity degree in 1944, six years before returning as a lecturer and meeting King as a student in 1950. After Crozer, Proctor became a John Price Crozer Fellow, studying ethics at Yale, while at the same time in 1945, becoming the pastor of Pond Street Baptist Church in Providence, Rhode Island. After a year at Yale, Proctor's journey took him to Boston University for doctoral studies, where he would graduate in 1950 with a doctorate in New Testament.

Proctor's stellar career as an academician and world-renowned Christian faith leader commenced after 1950, where doors of opportunity opened for both service and scholarship, each complementing the

---

18. Bond, 35.

other for significant social change. Proctor returned to his alma mater, Virginia Union University, as a professor in 1949, and within six years, he became the president in 1955. At Virginia Union, Proctor taught the future first African American governor of Virginia, Douglas Wilder, civil rights activist and pastor Wyatt Tee Walker, and Congressman Walter Fauntroy.[19] Proctor became the president of North Carolina A&T State University in 1960, where his outstanding work would gain him the favor of President John F. Kennedy.

One of Proctor's most notable stints of service was as director of the Peace Corps in Nigeria from 1963–1964 during Kennedy's administration. Sargent Shriver and President Kennedy convinced Proctor that a strong and intelligent Black man was needed in Africa to organize and "direct the huge cadre of white volunteers."[20] He was that person.

After his time with the Peace Corps, Proctor returned to his presidential post at North Carolina A&T State University for less than a year, before resigning and moving into full-time public service. Proctor served as the president for the National Council of Churches, president for the Institute for Service to Education, and special adviser for the Office of Economic Opportunity in the President Lyndon B. Johnson administration.[21] After a brief time on the faculty at the University of Wisconsin in 1968, Proctor joined the faculty at Rutgers University on a tenure-track appointment in 1969. He provided almost twenty years of service through the scholarship of teaching, preaching, and writing. Rutgers University named the Samuel D. Proctor Institute for Leadership, Equity, and Justice in his honor.[22]

Most notable of Proctor's life was his call to pastor the Abyssinian Baptist Church in the Harlem neighborhood of New York in 1972. Proctor succeeded the iconic Congressman, community leader, and pastor Adam Clayton Powell, Jr. In New York, Proctor was among the most notable preachers in the African American preaching tradition,

[19] Bond, 55.

[20] Samuel DeWitt Proctor, *The Substance of Things Hoped For: A Memoir of African-American Faith* (Valley Forge, PA: Judson, 1995), 100.

[21] *Rutgers Graduate School of Education, Samuel DeWitt Proctor Institute for Leadership, Equity, and Justice*, "About Samuel DeWitt Proctor," https://proctor.gse.rutgers.edu/content/about-samuel-dewitt-proctor%C2%A0.

[22] *Rutgers*, "About Samuel DeWitt Procter."

with Gardner C. Taylor, Sandy Ray, and William A. Jones. Space and word count will not allow a biographical sketch capturing Proctor's numerous awards, accolades, and ministerial accomplishments. Later in this chapter, I will examine his homiletical influence through social crisis preaching.

Helmut Thielicke

Thielicke was born in 1908 in Barmen, Germany. He was the son and grandson of educators. From his father, a teacher, and his grandfather, the headmaster of the Leibusch School at Wuppertal-Langerfeld, he gained a penchant for the life of the mind. From his mother, he inherited unwavering support in his ecclesiastical and professional pursuits and a deep faith that provided the resolve and resilience to stand against the pressures to succumb to the Third Reich and the nationalist church of Germany. Thielicke admits, "after the outbreak of the Third Reich my mother urged me to remain true to my convictions and to myself and not to give an inch to the Nazis."[23] That he did, without wavering, but it did not come without both a professional and personal cost.

Thielicke, from a young age, knew that he desired to study theology. His ambition to be a theologian was partly because "he perceived that it was the most learned and complex of all disciplines, and he was challenged by it."[24] During a conference in Wuppertal, before he finished high school, Thielicke, for the first time, heard Karl Barth, who profoundly solidified his quest to be a theologian of the church. He recounts, "This was when I totally lost my boyish heart to theology and applauded with such astonished enthusiasm that an elderly gentleman had to grab my knee to calm me down."[25] Though he would later oppose Barth on several theological conclusions, Barth inspired Thielicke to become the fertile intellectual seedbed from which theologically rich, yet practically relevant, arguments sprang.

During his early years—before his formal theological studies

[23.] Helmut Thielicke, *Note from a Wayfarer* (New York: Paragon, 1995), 16.

[24.] Robert Smith, Jr., "The Christological Preaching of Helmut Thielicke: The Theocratic Offices as a Paradigm for Preaching," (PhD diss., Southern Baptist Theological Seminary, 1993), 20.

[25.] Thielicke, 36.

began—Thielicke's parish afforded him weekly opportunities to hear social crisis preaching. His pastors, who were members of the Confessing Church, defied Hitler with prophetic urgency and energy. Thielicke states, "There references were made to the 'whore of Babylon' in an unmistakable allusion to the Nazi regime and its misdeeds."[26] Thielicke witnessed firsthand parish pastors who were committed to the Word of God and refused to capitulate to the ideology of the national church. These models left an indelible impression on him, as he would profoundly preach against the national church. Of Thielicke's prophetic preaching ministry, Dirks comments

> In pleading with ministers to proclaim the word and in denouncing them for their flight into liturgism, he speaks like a prophet. In criticizing the national church for its failings, he speaks like a prophet. When he raised questions about baptism, confirmation, and general church practices he is speaking like a prophet.[27]

Thielicke began his formal theological education at the University of Greifswald. His time at Greifswald would be short due to an almost unbearable illness when life-threatening complications would interrupt and prolong the completion of his studies. Thielicke's illness, an enlarged thyroid gland, led to numerous surgeries and procedures and required him to take medicines for the rest of his life. But it developed his faith and shaped his theology more than his university education did. He reflected on how his illness and suffering shaped his theology and faith: "I now knew what faith meant and everything that had previously fascinated me about theology was swept away by completely new impulses."[28]

Following Greifswald, Thielicke studied at Marburg, Erlangen, and Bonn. He wrote two doctoral dissertations for which he would receive doctorates in both philosophy and theology in 1931 and 1934, respectively. Even in doctoral studies, Thielicke encountered political opposition and resistance for his political views. The dean threatened

26. Thielicke, 38.
27. Dirks, *Laymen Look at Preaching*, 189 (see chap. 3, n. 19).
28. Thielicke, 66.

to reject both of his dissertations because they did not champion Nazism in them.[29] Thielicke believed that the unwarranted delays in the process were because of his theological positions as a Calvinist and as a "supporter of the Confessing Church, [who] ardently supported the 'Barmen Theological Declaration'."[30] But he would prevail; his dissertation was approved. During this time, Thielicke was married in 1937.

Thielicke's pastoral and academic positions brought him into unavoidable confrontation with the Nazi regime. The moral and academic undergirding of his home upbringing, his grave illness, the stellar intellectual models in his formal schooling and later in his university career, along with the uncompromising ethical examples of his pastoral influences, prepared him to endure the hardships that come with being a prophet of the Word of God. His faithfulness to the Word, and his commitment to preach it faithfully, raised the ire of the corrupt Nazi government. His ethics, shaped by Scripture, and his commitment to the faithful preaching of the Word, positioned him to be a model for social crisis preaching. Smith, Jr. writes, "His theology and ethics were sustaining notes that gave solidity to the whole of his preaching. He viewed theology and ethics as partners in the task of proclamation."[31] Preachers who dare confront society's ills must develop a social ethic that will help them preach the Word "in season and out of season" (2 Tim 4:2).

One of the first conflicts in his professional career was his dismissal from his teaching job at Heidelberg in 1940. His open criticism

---

[29.] A habilitation is similar to a doctoral dissertation. In Germany there was a system that required a habilitation for those who had completed the PhD or ThD, and who desired to teach, before they would be allowed a full professorship in a university. The habilitation had to be accepted by the university faculty and published as a way to establish oneself as an authority in a particular academic discipline.

[30.] Thielicke, 80. Note: The Barmen Declaration is a theological document drafted in 1934 by members of the Confessing Church, who resisted the German Christian movement, a tool of the government and a proponent of Nazi ideology. This document was not only a theological document, but it made a political statement as well. As Theses 6 of the declaration states, "The church should not be ruled by a leader ('Fuehrer'). There is no hierarchy in the church." The Barmen Declaration rejected the notion that the church was to be subordinate to the state, nor be a tool in the hands of the state. See Fred Dallmayr, ed., *The Legacy of the Barmen Declaration: Politics and the Kingdom* (Lanham: Lexington, 2019).

[31.] Robert Smith, "Helmut Thielicke: Between Pulpit and Lectern," December 1, 2009, *Crosswalk .com*, https://www.crosswalk.com/church/pastors-or-leadership/helmut-thielicke-between-pulpit -and-lectern-11605343.html.

of Nazism placed him on the regime's radar, where he became a constant target of their antagonism. Thielicke did a brief stint in the army before he was assigned a pastorate in Ravensburg in 1941. Shortly after, he became a lecturer and pastor in Stuttgart, where his preaching and teaching attracted thousands weekly. Thielicke's faithfulness as a pastor was personified during the war, as he ministered to his parishioners and shared in grief and loss. These kinds of experiences of communal sharing provide the social crisis preacher opportunities to infuse the social crisis sermon with the message of hope, redemptive suffering, and the role of the Holy Spirit to sustain us in suffering and grief.

Thielicke's life as a pastor and his life as a professor found harmonious symmetry. He describes the two as "indissolubly linked."[32] He established an adult Christian education program to instruct those who struggled to process the reality of God in a war-torn world. This cross section of the pastoral office and his professorial calling gave him insight about the need for making theological language understandable and relevant related to the everyday crises his students were suffering.

At Erlangen, Thielicke served as assistant to his former professor Paul Althaus, teaching introductory courses in theology. In 1936 he began teaching at Heidelberg until 1940, and like many prophetic preachers who have academic responsibilities, advocacy and activism emerge from the pulpit and the lectern. At Heidelberg, Professor Thielicke had run-ins with the Nazis, and as a result, he was censured for criticism of the Nazi's policy, then dismissed from his post as a professor.

After World War II, Thielicke accepted a professorship at the University of Tübingen to teach systematic theology, becoming rector of the university in 1951. In 1954, he joined the faculty at the University of Hamburg and became rector in 1960. In Hamburg, thousands of people flocked to hear Thielicke's preaching in multiple services on Saturdays and Sundays at the great Church of St. Michael. Hamburg would be Thielicke's final post as a university professor. He also had visiting professorships in New Zealand and Australia. Very few people who have worn the title of preacher, pastor, professor, administrator,

---

32. Thielicke, 285.

and author have had the homiletical impact and literary reach of Helmut Thielicke.

SMITH, PROCTOR, AND THIELICKE AS SACRED ANTHROPOLOGISTS

It is no secret that the prevailing crisis at the height of Proctor's and Smith, Sr.'s preaching ministries was the plight of African Americans and their fight for civil rights as citizens in the United States. As pastors, one would guess that many of the Sunday sermons from Abyssinian Baptist Church and First Baptist, Capitol Hill were geared towards instilling hope, resisting segregation and racism, and affirming the humanity of those in the pews. Thielicke had the pastoral responsibility of preaching and leading, according to Smith, Jr., "into three periods: The period prior to World War II (1928–1938); the period during World War II (1939–1945); and the period following World War II (1945–1986).[33]

In their role as pastors, they also fit the description of the sacred anthropologist: those who **recognize** their own presuppositions (about the biblical text and about people), while showing **respect** to their neighbor by **resisting** myths about their neighbor, and by serving as a **resource** of truth for their church and community, while challenging the congregation to **respond** by intentionally caring for and confronting the crises in their neighbor's community.

Recognizing Presuppositions

Smith, Sr., Proctor, and Thielicke were pastors who rooted their preaching ministries in the Bible. All three men lived and ministered when the church was under mounting pressure to endorse the culture's social standards and capitulate to the spirit of the age. For Thielicke, the strong Nazi state church exerted its mighty hand on all who resisted their ideology and worship of the Führer. Thielicke's guide was the Bible.

Both Smith, Sr. and Proctor, African American pastors and sons of

---

[33.] Robert Smith, Jr., "The Christological Preaching of Helmut Thielicke: The Theocratic Offices as a Paradigm for Preaching," (PhD diss., Southern Baptist Theological Seminary, 1993), 18.

the Black church, shared the experiences of segregation and discrimination with the members of the churches they served. But they did not agree with the Booker T. Washington model of Black leaders who advocated for a self-imposed separation of the races, nor did they give in to the separatist message and influence of Black nationalists.

Thielicke demonstrated a propensity for cultural intelligence during a visit to South Africa in 1959. He voiced strong opposition to apartheid, "inveighing vehemently against certain Boer Calvinist attempts to justify this racism with sham biblical support, and condemning the state guilty of this sin against humanity."[34] Thielicke was firm in his presupposition that the Bible did not support racial segregation and racial discrimination. Thielicke withstood cultural trends and religious bigotry from those who would use the Bible to support the inhumane treatment of native Africans. In a later visit to South Africa, he sought understanding and insight from "one of the most important leaders of the black opposition," citing that this scholar gave him "an insight above all into how apartheid affected individual families and the seething mentality of the younger generation."[35] Effective social crisis preaching requires that preachers gain cultural intelligence by listening and learning from the people most affected by social crises.

In 1986, at a preaching conference at Union Theological Seminary, Proctor gave a lecture entitled "Voice from Within," warning about the dangers of equating our confusing presuppositions with divine absolutes.[36] Proctor contends, "The culture we inherit is a strong force. We need to be careful that we do not equate our own cultural habits with the voice of God."[37] Proctor was also mindful of how cultural presuppositions could taint the sermon. He believed that presuppositions could be cloaked as our intuition or passed off as "the voice of God." To test our presuppositions, Proctor believes the preacher should "ask if what is said corresponds to the facts already in hand." This is excellent advice for our time. Lies, myths, misinformation, alternate facts, and politically polished presumptions abound among the members of our congregations. Myths circulate about the COVID-19 pandemic,

---

[34.] Thielicke, 334.
[35.] Thielicke, 335.
[36.] Proctor, *Preaching about Crises in the Community*, 10 (see chap. 4, n. 5).
[37.] Proctor, 69.

from the values and integrity of other cultures, to issues surrounding our nation's moral and religious legacy.

The question that needs to precede the social crisis sermon must be: "Is my information about this issue factual, and from what sources does it come?" Realizing that we have presuppositions, these three homiletical models remind us to submit to listening and learning, seeking the facts, and privileging the Bible as we depend on the Holy Spirit.

Unlike many secular critics and some Christian critics in America, Smith, Sr. did not alienate his hearers into racial factions or politically opposing tribes. He was a Christian who loved his country, and like a true prophet of God, out of that love, spoke against her sins. He did not absolve himself from the shortcomings of America by levying the responsibility of reconciliation and healing on the dominant population alone. From 1 Chr 16:29, Smith demonstrates this shared ownership in his sermon "Beauty," by proclaiming, "The trouble is that the heart of America is badly in need of being decorated with the beauty of holiness. Before these troubles of ours are overcome, we must work on the heart of America. And the heart of America is your heart and mine."[38] One must not assume that being American is the equivalent of being a Christian. While presupposition can be honorable and valuable, the wise social crisis preacher is aware of and sensitive to which presuppositions need to submit to the authority of the Word of God.

Respecting Neighbor

These social crisis preachers demonstrate the second component of the sacred anthropologist—respecting one's neighbor—by examining their theological assumptions concerning humanity. How those positive theological presuppositions are communicated through Christian proclamation, and lived out through their social engagement, reflects their theology. We have already discussed that the social crisis preacher embraces a theology that promotes the *imago Dei* in all humanity. We also contend that Christian proclamation is a viable means to address

---

[38]. Kelly Miller Smith, "Beauty," sermon, Vanderbilt University, Jean and Alexander Heard Library, Special Collections and University Archives, Kelly Miller Smith Papers, box 23, file 1.

the social crises concerning one's neighbor. Smith, Sr., Proctor, and Thielicke embraced these theological convictions, and they modeled this theology in life and preaching.

In Smith, Sr.'s powerful sermon from 1949, "The Relevance of the Ridiculous," taken from Matt 10:34–36, and given for a Brotherhood observance, he addresses the importance of every human to be recognized as a child of God in God's family, while he also calls out the bigotry of those who fail to acknowledge minorities as such:

> It is ridiculous to speak of a Brotherhood observance if it excludes other persons solely because of color and racial background. Here we have a serious paradox and we must recognize it as such. We must be fair enough in our thinking to realize that the building of brotherhood cannot be built upon a foundation of bias or prejudice. Actual brotherhood cannot exist if the feeling of oneness with the human family is absent. We gain nothing of permanent value by attempting to ignore that which constitutes the basic problem of America. If our religion does not address itself to our most serious problems, it is not much value to us. These are days when issues must be faced squarely, and those who are on the side of the aggressive love of Jesus must stand up and be counted.[39]

Proctor often preached to very diverse crowds. He often took his message of justice and equality for African Americans into all-white audiences in churches and schools. But Proctor is most known for his sermons challenging class division, economic exploitation, and apathy toward the poor. They reflect a sensitivity to the poor because Proctor believed that they were the ones the church should be most concerned about. Proctor's messages constantly reminded the church of her social responsibilities: "Just as the black church began to assert the dignity of all God's people, so the black church has had to be the unmuffled voice of social redemption in America across the years . . . .

[39.] Kelly Miller Smith Sr., "The Relevance of the Ridiculous," sermon, Vanderbilt University, Jean and Alexander Heard Library, Special Collections and University Archives, Kelly Miller Smith Papers, box 23, file 4.

The black church broods over the agony in our ghettos with dismay."[40] As a pastor in New York, Proctor was well aware of the plight in the urban ghettos, yet he did not look with condescension upon them, but with respect.

In his sermon entitled "Guilt and Destiny," from Gen 3:8–15, Thielicke demonstrates his respect for neighbor by calling attention to the Holocaust, where over six million Jewish people were killed at the hands of Thielicke's countrymen. In this sermon, Thielicke maintains that the cause of such atrocities lays at the feet of everyone. He proclaims,

> The very point of this ancient story is that it shows us that we put the question wrongly when we ask how evil came into the world. That is to say, when anybody asks the question in this way he is diverting attention away from himself. We had an impressive illustration of this after the collapse in 1945. Then the question was: Who was responsible for the millions of exterminated Jews, who was responsible for the brutalities of National Socialism in our own country and in occupied countries, who was responsible for Anne Frank, for the concentration camps, for Theresienstadt? Was not a people who would allow this bestial government to gain ascendancy among them dreadfully compromised? Was it not the fault of all of us that these hideous things could happen among us?[41]

Injustice often rolls into our corners of the world, one vote, one policy, and one executive order at a time. We all must feel some responsibility for the proliferation of the injustices and the social crises that creep slowly and subtly into our communities with dehumanizing power. When we fail to use our influence to win our golf partners, our classmates, our teachers, our church members, Facebook friends, our neighbors, and the strangers we meet, we are somewhat complicit in its proliferation. Respecting the neighbor means sharing in the responsibility of our neighbor's plight and developing the mind to

---

40. Samuel Proctor, *Samuel Proctor: My Moral Odyssey* , 157 (see chap. 3, n. 36).

41. Helmut Thielicke, *How the World Began* (Cambridge, UK: Lutterworth), p. 156, Kindle.

"care about and confront the crises in our neighbor's community in the power of the Holy Spirit."

Resisting Myths about One's Neighbor

Some social crises start as the flames of lies and myths are fanned. Social crisis preachers have the greatest opportunity to educate congregations about myths and lies associated with people and social issues. Thielicke preached when the Nazi government sought a pure white race—one that was not only European—but one in which there was no handicap, congenital disability, or any trait considered abnormal or weak. Thielicke's sermons aggressively, and many times at high cost to his liberty and opportunities, articulated that all men were created in the image of God. In his sermon, "Man, the Risk of God," based on Gen 1:26–31, he exhorts,

> This original design within us, on which I can count in myself and also in my neighbours, my colleagues, and my competitors, is described in our text from three points of view. First, we are created to have dominion over the earth. Second, we are made to live in the relationship of man and woman and thus are not designed to be soloists, but rather to live together with our fellow men. And third, we are images and likenesses of the divine being.[42]

At this writing, a global pandemic is wreaking havoc in a second wave. The Omicron variant of COVID-19 is responsible for rising numbers of deaths and hospitalizations, especially among unvaccinated people. All states are finally over the 50 percent fully vaccination rate.[43] While opinions and reasons abound as to why some states have lower COVID-19 vaccination rates than others, one reason should

---

[42.] Thielicke, 64.

[43.] See *Center for Disease Control and Prevention*, "COVID Data Tracker, COVID-19 Vaccinations in the United States," March 30, 2022, https://covid.cdc.gov/covid-data-tracker/#vaccinations_vacc-total-admin-rate-total. *The New York Times*, "See How Vaccinations Are Going in Your County and State," March 30, 2022, https://www.nytimes.com/interactive/2020/us/covid-19-vaccine-doses.html. Christopher Wolf and Adriana Rezal, "States with the Worst COVID-19 Vaccination Rates," March 24, 2022, *U.S. News & World Report*, https://www.usnews.com/news/best-states/articles/these-states-have-the-lowest-covid-19-vaccination-rates.

be taken out of the equation: false information and myths about the vaccine. The social crisis preacher is responsible for resisting political lies and myths. They are responsible for providing the flock of God with accurate and lifesaving information. In cases like this, incorporating advice or information from a medical professional into the sermon is wise. Likewise, as a part of the social crisis ministry, the sacred anthropologist can seek the help of a medical professional to deliver this information firsthand. At any rate, the sacred anthropologist should resist myths so that that truth will abound.

Smith, Sr. confronted the myth of racial inferiority in his life and ministry through the power of God's Word. He writes, "Because of the impact of that Word, the oppressed become aware that they are not hapless orphans deserted on the doorsteps of destiny, but are sons and daughters of a caring God."[44] With this emphasis on spiritual and cultural identity, the social crisis preacher in the Black church constructed a biblical worldview that countered the false worldview built upon flawed anthropology and manipulative theology. Smith, Sr.'s message does not ask the hearer to minimize or forfeit one's cultural identity to be accepted or appreciated, but rather to embrace one's ethnic and cultural being as part of God's family.

Smith, Sr. graciously confronted his congregation and Nashville citizens of every racial and denominational affiliation with the word of truth. In a baccalaureate address at Tennessee Agricultural & Industrial State College[45] on June 5, 1966, entitled "Stay Tuned for Another World," from Rev 21:1, Smith, Sr. proclaims, "The world which you are going to help create must be a place where men of all ethnic identities can walk the streets together as brothers. It must be a world where Negroes will not be relegated to certain carefully selected positions in our society and where black supremacy will be seen for the folly it truly represents."[46] In this message, Smith, Sr. challenges

---

[44.] Smith Sr., *Social Crisis Preaching*, 23 (see intro., n. 10).

[45.] The Tennessee Agricultural & Industrial State Normal School for Negroes University was founded in 1912. In 1925 it changed its name to Tennessee Agricultural and State Normal College, then to Tennessee Agricultural & Industrial State College. In 1968 it officially became Tennessee State University.

[46.] Kelly Miller Smith Sr., "Stay Tuned for Another World," baccalaureate address delivered at Tennessee A & I State University, June 5, 1966, Vanderbilt University, Jean and Alexander Heard Library, Special Collections and University Archives, Kelly Miller Smith Papers, box 23, file 6.

the spread of Black nationalism and the myth that Black supremacy was the answer to racism and discrimination. Additionally, Smith, Sr. challenges the segregationists who promoted the myth that the Bible forbids Black and white races to intermarry and to live in an integrated society.

There are instances when racial myths and lies are birthed from within a particular race about their own race. In chapter two, I discussed the myth of the curse of Ham theory, perpetrated to deny Black Americans the realization of their full humanity. Proctor was faithful in combatting both the myths of white supremacy and the lies of Black supremacy. In his memoir, *The Substance of Things Hoped For,* he provides commentary on how victims of racism, who use racial theories to prove that one's race is unique and superior, is wrong. In one example, Proctor criticizes a notable African American scholar, Leonard Jefferies, for perpetuating myths of Black superiority. Proctor comments, "We need to resist the appeal. Because similar anthropology and genetics have so often been used against us, I think most African Americans are uncomfortable with his arguments."[47] Sacred anthropologists resist any myths about humanity that teach that any race is inherently evil or more moral than any other.

Serving as a Resource

Smith, Sr. was resourceful. His resourcefulness came not only due to his social crisis preaching but also through the offerings of his social crisis ministry. Smith, Sr.'s involvement in desegregation prompted him to form the Nashville Christian Leadership Conference, an affiliate of the Southern Christian Leadership Conference, founded by King in 1957, after the Montgomery Bus Boycott's successful end on December 20, 1956. Nashville Christian Leadership Conference sponsored the sit-in training at his church, First Baptist Church, Capitol Hill. These sit-ins became pivotal instruments in the racial integration of Nashville's business establishments, whereby Smith, Sr., along with James Lawson, provided training according to the principles of nonviolent resistance propagated by Mahatma Gandhi.

[47.] Proctor, *The Substance of Things Hoped for,* 193 (see chap.5, n. 20).

During the early 1960s, sit-ins in Nashville became the model for sit-ins across the country. According to Barry Everett Lee, "the Nashville sit-in movement proved to be the most organized, disciplined, and effective sit-in campaign in the entire nation."[48] Lee further admits that the Nashville training model gave "Nashville cornerstone status in terms of the sit-ins."[49] Ultimately, these sit-ins, which targeted the lunch counters of the city's two largest department stores and four variety stores, were responsible for making Nashville the first major city in the South to integrate lunch counters on May 10, 1960.[50]

In their classic book, *We Have This Ministry,* Gardner C. Taylor and Proctor address the responsibilities of the pastor's vocation in detail. In his chapter entitled, "The Pastor as Teacher," Proctor writes, "The pastor as teacher has the rare privilege of being available to God's people as a resource, in whatever ways their lives may require assistance." Pastors who act as sacred anthropologists equip themselves to equip the body of Christ. In this role they must also possess the humility to direct church members and community members to other qualified individuals. Some examples are medical professionals, lawyers, credible websites, and other resources when their knowledge and expertise are insufficient to meet the cultural information required to mitigate the crisis. Proctor believed that teaching was a calling. And from that calling, he endeavored to be the resource that supplied the church and the nation with capable and able preachers who were equipped to deal with the plight of the Black community. Bond states,

---

[48.] Barry Everett Lee, "The Nashville Civil Rights Movement: A Study of the Phenomenon of Intentional Leadership Development and Its Consequences for Local Movements and the National Civil Rights Movement" (PhD diss., Georgia State University, 2010), 114.

[49.] Lee, 5.

[50.] Sit-ins were a nonviolent, direct-action tactic, mostly held at lunch counters, restaurants, and other business establishments that did not serve Blacks, or that did not serve Blacks as dine-in customers. Chet Huntley informs, "The sit-in is the dramatic spearhead of a changing mood, and behind it is the Negro's growing awareness of their economic power; the ultimate weapon in achieving, without violence, what they feel is their right. What we are witnessing is a new kind of militancy and with it a new kind of solider." Chet Huntley, *NBC White Papers #2*, produced by Al Wasserman for NBC, 1960, VHS provided by Kelly Miller Smith, Jr. This documentary, taped in 1960, focused on the sit-in movement in Nashville from the first sit-in, in February 1960 to April 19, 1960. This documentary featured footage of actual sit-ins, interviews from Kelly Miller Smith, Sr. and the student activists, as well as white citizens who supported integration and desegregation. Interviews from Nashville's segregationist politicians, citizens who supported segregation, as well as business owners who were proponents of segregation, were also in the footage.

Proctor wanted to produce public theologians, black public theologians specifically, who would discern the ills of the American environment and proclaim a truth that would resolve the problems in the black community and in the world. Proctor spent the last years of his career teaching at seminaries, preaching at churches across the nation, and giving lectures at black and white preaching functions and religious conventions.[51]

In the Black church, discipleship often looks like this. It is developing congregations to follow Jesus's example of love and advocacy for minorities and the marginalized.

Thielicke's life was also a resource. The cultural milieu in which he found himself mandated that his preaching and teaching be an alternative to the heretical teachings of the state church of Germany. When he was unable to accept a pastoral post to Fredrich Schleiermacher's pulpit at Trinity Church in Berlin due to travel restrictions levied against him for his anti-Nazi views,[52] Thielicke formed a public adult Christian education initiative that promoted faith education, with a focus on "a war-torn country and how God was relevant to their crisis situation and everyday problems."[53] There are times when the sacred anthropologist must offer a truthful counternarrative when sociopolitical forces hijack the church's message. Smith, Sr., Proctor, and Thielicke served as educators and used the lectern as an extension to shape and develop people, future pastors, and the next generation of scholars. I find the bivocational model of being a professor and pastor complementary roles in combatting social crises and instilling hope. The classroom develops a life of the mind; the sanctuary develops spiritual formation.

[51.] Bond, *The Imposing Preacher*, 149.

[52.] Friedrich Daniel Schleiermacher (1768–1834) is considered the father of modern liberal theology, as well, as the father of modern hermeneutics. Born in Breslaw, Germany, Schleiermacher become one of the most influential theologians and philosophers of the eighteenth and early nineteenth centuries. His most notable work, *On Religion: Speeches to Its Cultured Despisers* was published in 1799 and is known for reconciling Enlightenment criticism with orthodox Protestantism. Schleiermacher is a highly regarded authority in hermeneutics and ethics. See *Stanford Encyclopedia of Philosophy*, "Friedrich Daniel Ernst Schleiermacher," August 8, 2017, https://plato.stanford.edu /entries/schleiermacher/and Friedrich Schleiermacher, Tran. John Oman, *On Religion: Speeches to Its Cultured Despisers*, (London: K. Paul, Trench, Trubner & Co., Ltd., 1893).

[53.] Robert Smith, Jr., "The Christological Preaching of Helmut Thielicke: The Theocratic Offices as a Paradigm for Preaching," (PhD diss., Southern Baptist Theological Seminary, 1993), 27.

Challenging People to Respond

Social crisis preachers, as sacred anthropologists, must be intentional in mobilizing the people in the pews to move from being stoic spectators to active participants in God's work to dismantle systems of injustice and bring forth structures that ensure fairness and flourishing for the least of these. Preaching that addresses the social results of the infiltration of sin in our world requires people to do something. For instance, the social crisis ministry and movement in Nashville, Tennessee, during the 1960s were the result of Smith, Sr.'s social crisis preaching. Those who heard his sermons responded proactively by inviting the dominant group to participate in the shared fellowship of all God's children. Smith, Sr.'s messages often informed the dominant group that they were out of line with God's intended purposes for humanity.

Again, Smith, Jr. reports, "Thielicke's sermons advocated a social action aspect which emphasized uplifting his people."[54] During his second tour in America, Thielicke challenged Christians in the United States in 1963 to speak out against segregation in American cities and begin in the church. He states,

> And here certainly it is the individual Christian who is challenged, the individual who in his place in life meets his neighbor of another colour. But I believe that the church as an institution also must not remain silent. As the church of the Word it must break the silence about these things. We can have all kinds of objections to the racial laws in many regions of Africa; but at least such laws are open and clear. You know where you are, and when you discuss these questions you need only to cite the laws. That in America the situation is different on this point distresses me very much just because I love this country. Here there are collective unspoken agreements. People know what the democratic ethos demands and therefore human rights are established on paper. In reality, however, it is often quite otherwise. . . . Therefore in my judgment one of the first small steps would be for the church

---

[54.] Smith, Jr., 55.

of Christ to do away with racial segregation in its own ranks. This gives us a task which we can perform; this is not some big program which exceeds our ability to fulfill.[55]

Here is a lesson for our age. Although we would be hard-pressed to find many churches in the United States with visible signs that segregate people in the pews by race, there are churches that are segregated in their worship styles, leadership, and the causes they champion. There are still churches in America that are silent on racial injustice and the insidious, hidden effects of past and current race prejudice. Although racial segregation is almost a long-gone reality, there are still denominations and churches in America where the pews are filled with Latino, African American, Hispanic, and Asian worshipers. Still, few of these qualified, credentialed, and faithful Christians hold positions of authority in these churches and denominations. Today, there is segregation among the leadership of our churches. As Thielicke did in 1963, we must today; we must speak out.

CONCLUSION

Through their sermons and writings, Smith, Sr., Proctor, Thielicke serve as exemplar social crisis preachers. As faithful pastors, they embody the tenets that describe a sacred anthropologist. Another crucial lesson these models teach us is that social crisis preaching is a lifestyle. Much like Smith, Sr.'s "pre- and post-proclamation function," the most essential component of the social crisis sermon is the preacher's function and engagement in social crises before a word is written from the study or uttered from the pulpit. Social crisis preaching is not bound to the pulpit. The sermon is strengthened and made effective by what the preacher does in the community and among the people before and after.

Moreover, these three models demonstrate that social crisis preaching uses various media. Today's social crisis preacher must consider using

---

[55.] Helmut Thielicke, "Racial Integration and the Christian: The Problem of the Political Engagement of the Church," *Between Heaven and Earth: Conversations with American Christians,* (UK: Lutterworth, 1964), Kindle, chap. 7, Location 2138.

social media, blogs, podcasts, and articles, as well as pulpit ministry, to address social crises through the gospel of Jesus Christ. Preaching Christ is the proclamation of God's radical answer to sin, the root cause of social crises. Thielicke, Smith, Sr., and Proctor are noteworthy models.

CONCLUSION

Marvin McMickle declares, "Prophetic preaching points out a lack of concern and acquiescence in the face of evil that can so easily replace the true God of Scripture who calls true believers to the active pursuit of justice and righteousness for every member of society."[56] Social crisis preaching is precisely concerned with the pursuit of justice and righteousness of every member of our world. There are times when the spiritual decay of our community reaches such depths that the social conditions in which we live reach crisis proportions. In these times our proclamation must address those crises through the lens of the Bible, with clear and relevant ethical application. Social crisis preaching is Christian proclamation that develops congregations to intentionally care about and confront the social crises in their neighbor's community in the power of the Holy Spirit. May every herald of the gospel be faithful in this sacred endeavor.

[56.] Marvin McMickle, *Where Have All the Prophets Gone? Reclaiming Prophetic Preaching in America* (Cleveland: Pilgrim, 2006), chap. 1, Kindle.

NAME & SUBJECT INDEX

134, 141–43, 152, 180
hope, 23, 50, 99, 122, 139
Hosea, 150
House, Paul, 38–39
housing discrimination, 4, 81, 114–15
Howard, John, 55–58
Hubbard, Robert L. Jr., 64
humanism, 63
humility, 176
Huntley, Chet, 176
Hurricane Katrina, 139

I

identity, 49–50
idolatry, 30–31, 33
Ignatieff, Michael, 55–56
image-bearers, 15–16, 170–71
image of God, 15, 62, 87, 173
immigration, 87, 108–9
institutional injustice, 4–5
interdisciplinary content, 99, 116–18, 128
interpretation, 26, 70, 73, 77
interpretive communities, 66, 98
interrupting justice, 92–93
Ivory, Luther D., 18

J

Jean, Botham, 40–42
Jean, Brandt, 41–42
Jefferies, Leonard, 175
Jeremiah, 150
Jernigan, Dustin, 89, 90
Jeter, Joseph R. Jr., 97
Jim Crow laws, 24, 82, 157
John Chrysostom, 143
Johnson, Lyndon B., 163

Johnson, Mordecai, 158
Jones, Absalom, 65
Jones, William A., 164
Jowett, J. H., 104, 160
judgment, 38–39
Juneteenth, 88–89
justice, 6, 8, 16, 34–37, 39–43, 54, 65, 109, 144, 157, 171, 180

K

Karni, Annie, 88
Kennedy, John F., 163
Kim, Matthew D., 66, 74, 76
Kindelan, Katie, 88
King, Martin Luther Jr., 11, 18, 24, 47–48, 51, 54, 145, 147–48, 158, 162, 175
kingdom of God, 38, 54, 109
Klein, William W., 64
Koren, Marina, 122
Kuruvilla, Abraham, 52, 101

L

lament, 90–91
language, 50–51, 99, 118–20, 128
LaRue, Cleophus J., 66–67
Lathrop, Breanna, 97
Lawson, James, 159, 175
Lee, Barry Everett, 176
Lee, Opal, 88
Lewis, John, 159
liberation, 10, 14, 70, 83
liberation theology, 11–14
Litfin, Duane, 142–43
logos, 144, 146–47
Long, Thomas G., 21–22, 31, 103, 112
Loury, Glenn, 82

SCRIPTURE INDEX

2 Chronicles
9:8   *35*

Ezra
3:8–13   *116*

Nehemiah
4:4–5   *39*

Esther
2:20b   *91*
3   *24*
3:1   *92*
3:2   *92*
3:10   *92*
3:12–14   *92*
4:1b   *90*
4–8   *92*
7:3–4   *91*
8:3–12   *92*
9:20–28   *89*
9:28b   *90*
9:31   *90*

Psalms
8:4–8   *38*
12:5   *104*
35:9–10   *104*
37:28   *39*
89:14   *35, 39*
103:3   *104*
109:2–3   *104*
113:5–8   *104*
123   *102*
140:1–2   *104*
140:12–13   *104*

Proverbs
6:16–19   *39*
11:1   *39, 43*
13:11   *31*
14:31   *31*
14:34   *39, 86*
21:15   *39*
22:4   *103*
22:9   *31*
22:16   *31*
28:25   *31*
29:7   *31*

Isaiah
28:6   *39*
33:5   *35*
33:7–10   *38*
53:4a   *145*
55:11   *119*
61:3   *91*
66:2   *28*

Jeremiah
9:1–2a   *150*
9:24   *39*
17:9   *11*
20:9   *150*

Ezekiel
3:15b   *19*
34:16   *39*

Daniel
3   *43*
3:1–7   *11*

16:1–13 *120*
18:1–8 *43*
19 *43*
23:6–25 *11*
24:1–7 *116*

John
1:14 *19*
5:1–14 *72*
6:1–7 *24*
6:1–14 *102*
12:8 *12*
13:34 *75*
14:9 *16*
15:19 *108*

Acts
2 *84*
2:44–46 *31*
5 *24*
5:29 *33*
8:27 *84*
10 *24*
10:1–35 *140*
10:34 *50*
14 *143*
16:25–28 *140*
17 *143*
17:26–28 *38*
17:26a *71*
17:28 *62*

Romans
1:21 *11*
5 *62*
5:12 *25*
6:1–4 *41*

8:18–25 *38*
12:1–2 *11*
12:2 *108*
12:15 *91*
12:19b *43*
14:1–15:13 *38*

1 Corinthians
1:17 *143*
2:1–5 *143*
3:6 *143*

2 Corinthians
4:7–18 *102*
5:17 *62, 108*
11:6 *143*

Galatians
1:4 *10*
1:4b *20*
2 *24*
2:10 *31*
5:6 *122*
5:22–23 *2*
6:2 *139*

Ephesians
1:4a *152*
1:16 *152*
2:6b *152*
2:10b *152*
2:14 *21*
2:15b–16 *14*
4:12 *133*
4:22 *11*
5:21 *101*
5:22–6:4 *140*